POOR CECCO

Harlequin
Lion
Anna
Easter chicken
Gladys
Virginia May
Cecco
Money pig
Tubby
Bulka
ida
EXPRESS WAGON 51

POOR CECCO

The wonderful story of a wonderful dog who was the jolliest toy in the house until he went out to explore the world

BY

MARGERY WILLIAMS BIANCO

and introduced by MARGERY FISHER

illustrated by

Antony Maitland

ANDRE DEUTSCH

This edition published 1973 by
André Deutsch Limited
105 Great Russell Street
London WC1

First published in Great Britain 1925 by Chatto & Windus Ltd.

Printed in Great Britain by Cox & Wyman Ltd
London Fakenham and Reading

ISBN 0 233 96467 3

CONTENTS

TO

PAMELA AND CECCO

Whose book this is

POOR CECCO

Introduction by Margery Fisher

SHIPS' libraries are far from satisfying to a voracious child reader. When I emigrated to New Zealand with my parents in 1922 I was lost without my own books and the library was little help. Then one day I picked up a magazine and it fell open at an exciting picture of a black cat pushing a stuffed dog down a crack in a huge, gnarled willow tree. It was a Rackham picture. The tree had all the sinister life of the elms in *Peter Pan in Kensington Gardens*, a favourite book of mine at the time; the cat, Murrum, looked fascinatingly wicked. Captured by the picture, I was soon totally captivated by the story. In the next few days I managed to find all the instalments from the beginning up to the kidnapping of Tubby. It was agonising not to know how the story ended and I spent weeks writing down what I could remember and trying to finish it. It never occurred to me that there might be a way to trace the story or that it might later be published as a book. I hardly noticed the author's name.

Gradually I forgot about the heroic wooden dog and the sinister cat. Years later I was looking up *The Velveteen Rabbit* in the British Museum catalogue when I saw an entry for a book called *Poor Cecco.* Something stirred at the back of my mind. I ordered the book and found the Rackham picture. Half an hour later I knew, at last, how the story ended.

Reading *Poor Cecco* now is, for me, rather like listening to a long-playing record of a work known for years as a seventy-eight. I still hear the pause where, as it were, a record had to be turned over, the point where, forty years ago, the story broke off. I can never feel quite the same about the finding of the treasure or the wedding of Tubby and Bulka as I do about Cecco's journey and his meeting with the redoubtable wooden doll Jensina. Still, this remains for me the best of all toy stories.

Cecco and Bulka and the rest of the toys belonged to Margery Bianco's children and it seems natural to guess that their saga began as a continuous bedtime story, like the tales of Pooh, Piglet and Eeyore. Whether or not this is so, the group of stories which Margery Bianco wrote about the toys did not appear in print till after her children had left the nursery; they grew out of affectionate memory. Margery Williams, born in London, the daughter of a barrister who was a distinguished classical scholar, had been taken to America first when she was nine and over the years this became her home rather than England. She began writing in her 'teens but stories for children came a long time later – after marriage and the First World War and a long period of no writing. Her daughter Pamela, whose artistic talent had been evident when she was very young, had an exhibition of paintings in London not long after the war and Mrs Bianco went to England with her. She wrote later:

> 'I wanted to write again, but I disliked everything I had written before. I wanted to do something different, but did not know what it should be. So I wrote *The Velveteen Rabbit*, and by a sort of accident it became the beginning of all the stories written since. For by thinking about toys and remembering toys they became suddenly very much alive – Poor Cecco and Tubby and all the family toys that had been

so much a part of our lives. Toys I had loved when I was a little girl: my almost forgotten Fluffy, who was the Rabbit, and old Dobbin the skin horse.'

Memory is one clue to the 'sort of accident' that produced *The Velveteen Rabbit*, *The Little Wooden Doll*, *The Skin Horse* and *Poor Cecco*. There are perhaps other clues too. In the 1920s, when the stories were written, every thinking man and woman had to come to terms with an alarming increase in mass production, of material things and of opinions. Through the adventures of toys whose personalities had been shaped in the nursery years Margery Bianco found a way to state her belief in the quality of life. It was no accident that one of them, Andy, formed the 'Brotherhood of Ancient Toys' to stand against the influence of the 'Fiventen'. The velveteen rabbit came to life to demonstrate the value of love and kindness, as a counter to materialism. When a new edition of the story appeared in England in 1970 its reception proved that the message was still valid. And though *Poor Cecco* is to all intents and purposes an engagingly simple adventure story, its wooden hero communicates the need for courage and love in a world beset with enemies.

The velveteen rabbit imagined that things were 'real' if they had 'things that buzz inside you and a stick-out handle'; the skin horse advised him that he could become real only when a child loved him. The toys in *Poor Cecco* – the snobbish dolls, sentimental Tubby, even Ida Down, so sympathetic and so thoroughly sat-upon by the rest – are real for this reason too, especially Cecco, who was affectionately neglected. 'Being made of wood, it didn't much matter if he was left out in the rain all night' . . . but as a corollary, 'he rarely came to grief, for he was the cleverest of all the toys'.

Personality has grown quite naturally out of the physical appearance of the toys. Wood is a steadfast, reliable material: so is Cecco. Bulka's lumpy stuffed body, with the stitches constantly coming undone, matches his impetuous, accident-prone character, his outbursts of crying that sound like 'a sad five-finger exercise'. The book sparkles with the fun of childhood play and its special logic. When Tubby and Bulka are married, the list of presents is exquisitely right, beginning with Poor Cecco's last penny and ending with the house-mice who 'brought seven thimblefuls of rice, a perfectly good cheese rind and a long pin with a pink head, which they had found under the floor-boards'.

This is the reality of the nursery and the toy-cupboard. When Cecco and Bulka set out on the early morning walk that turns into such an adventure, the story reaches out to the Pennsylvania of Margery Bianco's childhood. The toys walk on equal terms with animals and villagers alike, in a landscape as credible as it is magical. Without question they can accept a lift from a countryman on his way to market and find shelter in a woodchuck's hole. All through the story, in fact, Margery Bianco enjoys contriving situations in which they can behave like people. When gypsy-born Jensina comes back with Cecco to join the nursery family, Gladys and Virginia May receive her with the hauteur of spoiled society ladies. Noticing that Jensina's shoes are painted on, they invite her maliciously to take them off; but Jensina sees that the dolls have lost their own shoes and that one of Virginia's feet is broken, and retorts 'I never take my shoes off in company. I don't think it is quite nice'. Like Rumer Godden's doll stories, *Poor Cecco* is a comic novel in miniature.

Anne Carroll Moore commented, reviewing the book when it first appeared, 'It is this sure sense of the personalities of her characters, whether toys or living creatures, and her complete grasp of dramatic requirements that give Mrs Bianco's work an assured high place among children's stories.' *Poor Cecco* is a short book, moving along with grace and simplicity, but it is most skilfully plotted. The feeling of improvisation essential to the description of a journey is backed by a careful arrangement of events. The danger that threatens from Murrum the prowling cat is balanced by the danger that threatens Jensina when she carries off the ancestral treasure of the rats, the

Tooth of Grimalkin, and the two plots run easily together to bring the tale to its joyous conclusion. Most of all the continuity of the tale depends on the limpid, incisive, beautifully judged prose, with its echoes of Hans Andersen and Beatrix Potter and its own special civilised music.

A few years after *Poor Cecco* was published in book form, Margery Bianco reviewed a picture-book she had known as a child, and remarked that 'the impression of picture-books seen and handled in early years remains always vivid and intense, so much so that to open one again after a lapse of years is an actual shock, so violently is one precipitated backward into one's past'. She might be writing of my own experience with the 'wonderful story of a wonderful wooden dog who was the jolliest toy in the house until he went out to explore the world'.

Rackham's half-dozen colour plates were so much a part of the story for me that I was sad to hear that these were not available for the reprint – sad, at least, until I saw Antony Maitland's drawings. Preserving the appearance of the actual toys of the Bianco nursery, as seen in Rackham's illustrations, he has indicated their personalities with a shrewd and tender humour – even to those minor but important characters, the sentimental Lion and the inquisitive Easter Chick. As for his country scenes, they take you right into a fresh morning world where Cecco, Bulka and Jensina are completely at home.

I can imagine no more delightful or authentic interpretation of *Poor Cecco*. I have never been able to understand how a story so good could have gone underground for so many years; now, no child need miss the vivid pleasure of reading it.

CHAPTER I

How Murrum shut the toy-cupboard door

DONG!

That is the old clock in the hall striking midnight. A tall old clock with a round foolish face. He always looks surprised, though he ought to know perfectly well what the hour is. 'Dong!' he says. 'Another thirty minutes gone! Now, how did that happen?'

It is so still that the voice of the old clock can be heard all through the house. Upstairs, where the children are asleep; out in the kitchen, where the mice run to and fro on the floor – even outside on the doorstep, where Murrum, the black cat, sits in a square of moonlight washing his paws.

Murrum is not so old as the clock, but he knows far more; in fact, he knows everything. He knows where all the birds' nests are, and who just rang the doorbell, and what the family are going to have for dinner. He knows why the cream disappears and what happened to cook's silver thimble and just where Boodles buried his last hambone. He knows all these things and a great deal more, but he doesn't go about chattering. He leaves that to the sparrows and the house-mice, who spread all the gossip between them. Murrum sits and washes his paws.

The moonlight is white on the doorstep and Murrum is black, but there is a white patch just under his chin, and he has four white mittens. He washes and washes, down his nose and over his ears and round his ears, and while he washes he smiles.

'I've fixed them this time!' says Murrum.

'Fixed what?'

Murrum stops washing and stares down with his pale insolent eyes.

It is Toad, the old night-watchman, with his brown wrinkled coat and speckled vest. He comes out from under the doorstep, blinks up through his gold spectacles and grunts. 'Fixed what?' he says again.

'Mind your own business!' says Murrum.

'It is my business!' said the Toad. 'Everything's my business. I wish it wasn't. I have too much to look after, that's what it is! It keeps me on the hop the whole time. Dearie me, what's all that noise?'

There was certainly a commotion going on indoors. Bumping and thumping and clattering, and with it the queerest little shrieks and howls. Muffled noises, as though a number of small people were shut up together in a box and were extremely angry about it. One voice, louder than the rest, that sounded like a very sad five-finger exercise.

Murrum listened, his head turned to one side and one paw still lifted.

'A fine rage they're in, aren't they!' said Murrum. 'That'll teach them to spoil my mousing!'

'Dearie me,' said the Toad, 'what have you been up to now? Who is doing all that squealing?'

'Why, the toys, to be sure!' said Murrum. 'A wretched noisy crowd they are, night after night prancing and singing all over the house! The place isn't fit to live in. There's three nights now I haven't caught a single mouse, with their carryings on. No sooner do I get to work and settle down, all in position, nicely balanced, than – bing! – in they start with their noise, and I have to begin all over again. It's enough to make one a nervous wreck. But I've settled them to-night. I turned the button on the toy-cupboard door and now they can't get out.'

The Toad pushed back his spectacles and scratched his head 'They'll be terribly angry!' he said at last.

'Let them be angry!' said Murrum. 'Who cares for that? What sensible people see in those things I can't imagine! The best of them isn't worth three hairs off a kitten's tail. There's that Anna, with her stupid face, and the rag doll, and Bulka, that you can't so much as look at but he starts squealing, and Harlequin, that thinks he's so wonderful – a stupid lot, I call them! And as for that loose-jointed thing like a dog, that they call Poor Cecco, always poking about where he isn't wanted, he's the worst of the lot! Ugh! I can't stand the sight of him!'

'Still,' said the Toad, 'you shouldn't have locked them up in the cupboard. That's going too far. You could be had up for that!'

'I don't care!' said Murrum. 'I do what I like and I go where I choose! And now I'm off to keep my appointment!'

And he gave a last look at his coat, all smooth and glossy, stretched out his ten white toes on the doorstep, and arched his back.

Now all the while Murrum was talking someone had been creeping very slowly along the edge of the porch just over Murrum's head. He had to move rather stiffly and carefully because he was all made of wood, and if he once let his joints rattle there would be a terrible noise. So he went gently – clop – clop – and when he reached the big flower-pot that stood just by the doorstep he folded his hind legs under him and lay down, with one ear cocked up, to hear what was going on. For Murrum hadn't been quite as clever as he thought he

was, and when he shut the toy-cupboard door Poor Cecco wasn't inside at all.

In fact it very seldom happened, as Murrum might have remembered if he hadn't been in such a hurry, that Poor Cecco did get put away with the other toys when the nursery was tidied at night. Poor Cecco had been through many adventures and was well able to look after himself, and, being made of wood, it didn't much matter if he was left out in the rain all night, so nobody troubled very much about him. And if any one did happen to want Poor Cecco the best sort of place to look for him, at any time, would be out in the garden or under the bureau or down behind the woodbox in the back kitchen. Once indeed he nearly got thrown on the fire by mistake, only Cook recognised him just in time. Sometimes he would disappear for days at a stretch and then turn up where you least expected him, in the laundry basket, or poked away under the sofa cushions. But with all his irregular habits he rarely came to grief, for he was the cleverest of all the toys.

He stayed quite still now behind the flower-pot and listened to what Murrum had to say.

'Ah, there's nothing like being popular in society!' sighed the Toad. 'Now, with me it's work – work all the time!'

Murrum wasn't listening. He came down from the doorstep, still stretching himself and yawning very delicately so as to show the inside of his pink mouth. Standing in the moonlight, he began to make camels, humping his back and waving his long tail from side to side while he admired his shadow on the ground. But just as he was nicely balanced on tiptoe, making the last and most beautiful camel of all, Poor Cecco wriggled out from behind the flower-pot, took a flying jump and landed, with all his joints rattling, right on Murrum's nose!

Murrum gave one terrible yowl and flew off down the garden path and over the wall, with his tail as big as a saucepan handle.

Poor Cecco lay on the ground and laughed, all his four legs sprawling and one ear still cocked up.

'Where did you come from?' asked the Toad, rubbing his head, which Poor Cecco had narrowly escaped kicking.

'Hinksman!' said Poor Cecco, which means: 'I won't tell you!'

'I suppose you think that's clever!' said the Toad, still rubbing his head, for he was quite annoyed, and moreover his spectacles had nearly dropped off with fright. 'Respectable people hop on the ground, and don't go dropping out of the skies like that. If you think you're an aeroplane say so at once, and then at least one is warned!'

And he turned his back and began to shuffle away along the edge of the flower-border.

'Don't be in such a hurry!' said Poor Cecco.

But the Toad made no answer. He was already late on his evening rounds. Poor Cecco stood up and shook himself.

'And now, I suppose,' he said, 'I had better go and let them out!'

CHAPTER 2

The treasure hunt

THERE had been a fine racket going on in the toy-cupboard all this while. But by the time Poor Cecco had trotted round to the back of the house and climbed in through the kitchen window, most of the toys had given up thumping and shouting and were sitting still there in the dark, tired out and very cross. Only the noise like a five-finger exercise still kept on. Poor Cecco could hear it quite distinctly as he poked his head through the kitchen window. 'Uh-huh! Uh-huh! Uh-huh! Uh-huh!'

That was Bulka, the rag puppy. Bulka had been mended and re-stitched so many times that he had almost lost his original shape and he really looked more like a pin cushion than a dog. He always cried in tune – the tune of a five-finger exercise – which annoyed the rest of the toys so much that they would do anything rather than hear Bulka cry. The worst of it was that, being an extremely sensitive person, he cried far oftener than there was any need to, whenever anything went wrong, for instance, or especially if his feelings were hurt; and then all the other toys were obliged to stuff their fingers in their ears and run away until Bulka was comforted. They simply couldn't stand it, but they had to stand it now, for there they were all shut up together and Bulka had been crying steadily for at least three-quarters of an hour, ever since Murrum fastened the toy-cupboard door, and all they could do was to stuff their fingers in their ears as tightly as possible and try to pretend they didn't hear him.

But at the sound of Poor Cecco's feet – clop – clop – along the passage and across the floor, Bulka stopped crying at once, right in the middle of his tune, and his companions immediately unstopped their ears to listen. The toy-cupboard was quite low, built in next to the fireplace as in all proper houses, so all Poor Cecco had to do was to reach up on his hind legs and turn the button round again.

Out they all tumbled, all talking at once and very excited. First came Bulka, who had his nose to the crack in the door all the evening, and close at his heels came Tubby, who was a little bigger than Bulka and looked very much like him, except that her ears were longer and her eyes were rounder. Then Gladys and Virginia May, hand in hand, Gladys wearing a white satin petticoat and the wedding veil in which she had been married to Harlequin the week before, and which was really only loaned to her. Virginia wore nothing; all her clothes were in the wash.

Next came Harlequin himself, all covered with spangles, exclaiming 'Hey Presto!' He looked quite fine if you half-closed one eye, so as not to see where the stitches were coming undone. After him came the Easter Chicken and the Lion and the wooden Engine, and then Anna the lamb, with a bell round her neck and the little green meadow, that she always carried about with her, fastened under her feet. Last of all was Ida, because she could never get up until the others had moved first. Ida's last name was Down; she was flat and square, dressed in pink satin with a silk cord all round.

All the small toys stayed in the bottom of the cupboard. They were already tired and had gone to sleep.

'Now,' cried Poor Cecco. 'What shall we do?'

'Let's have a picnic!' said Tubby.

Harlequin wanted to punish Murrum, but no one knew where he was. Engine and the Chicken were talking together, and as usual the Lion was flirting with Anna; they didn't mind what was done so long as someone decided quickly. Ida thought it was time to have another wedding, but it was now Virginia's turn to be married, and Virginia May refused. She had no wedding clothes, since Gladys would not give up the veil, and the only person they could think of for her to marry was Bulka, whom she couldn't endure. Meantime Bulka and Tubby were quarrelling because Bulka said that Tubby's picnics were always stupid and Tubby called Bulka a cry-baby.

Anna said: 'Well, if nobody's willing to do anything—'

Poor Cecco jumped up and banged on the table. 'I know what let's do,' he said. 'Let's go on a treasure hunt!'

'What's that?' they all cried.

'It's got to be out of doors,' said Poor Cecco, explaining very rapidly, 'and we take the express wagon to bring it back in, and you find a place where someone has buried treasure and you dig it up and divide it. I'm going to do the digging.'

'How do you find the place?' Harlequin asked.

'There are lots of places,' said Poor Cecco. 'You measure the ground and then you dig. Generally it's under a big stone.'

Bulka remembered a big stone down by the end of the garden. There might be treasure there. But how could one tell?

You couldn't tell. If you knew beforehand, Poor Cecco said, then there was no sense in looking and it wouldn't be a treasure hunt. Any-

one might do that. But you had to have spades, and he sent Tubby to fetch a tin spade and a broken spoon that were in the bottom of the toy-cupboard.

The express wagon had gone to sleep. He grumbled terribly when they woke him up. 'I work all day,' he complained, 'and at night I want to be quiet. I wish you'd think of something with a boat in it for a change!'

But Tubby had returned with the spade, and everyone climbed in, paying no attention to his protests. They spread Ida on the bottom of the wagon first, and all sat on her to keep their feet warm. At the last moment space had to be made for the Money-Pig, who insisted on coming too. The word 'treasure' was quite enough to rouse him up.

'He thinks we're going to find money, and he's afraid he won't get any!' whispered Tubby to Gladys, snuggling up close against her in the wagon. 'He's an awful miser. Did he give you a wedding present last week?'

'He did not,' said Gladys.

'When I marry,' said Tubby, spreading her skirts out, 'I shall be married in Tubbyland and I shall have a Tubbyland wedding. Everyone will give me presents. I shall wear a long satin train and roses and a blue veil.'

Bulka was staring gloomily in front of him. 'You'll look awfully stupid!' he said.

. . . . and dumped them, suddenly and unexpectedly.

'Anyway,' said Tubby angrily, 'I shan't ask *you!* When is the wagon going to start?'

They were waiting for Anna, who, as usual, had a piece of string tangled round her wheels. Anna had to walk alongside, for they wouldn't let her bring her meadow into the wagon, and she refused to leave it behind.

'Anna is so silly!' murmured Virginia May, watching Anna lift first one foot and then the other, very affectedly, while Poor Cecco got the string unwound. 'It's absurd to be so attached to a little piece of ground like that. It isn't as if anything grew on it. She just likes to pretend she's an heiress and landowner, so as to make a wealthy marriage. But nothing will ever come of it, mark my word!'

They started off – rattle – rattle – rattle – through the back entry and down the garden path. It was a very bumpy ride. The express wagon felt too drowsy to look where he was going. Moreover he was still quite cross and so didn't mind how much he shook them all up.

Rattle! Now they were going round and round the strawberry bed. At each turn the wheels lifted up, nearly spilling them out. Anna, who tried to keep pace with them, kept on tripping. 'Stop!' cried Poor Cecco. 'This isn't the way!'

But the express wagon laughed a nasty laugh.

'You woke me up for your pleasure,' he declared, 'and now I shall go where I choose for mine! And I choose to go round and round the strawberry bed!'

But in the end he grew tired of it and dumped them all, suddenly and unexpectedly, on a border of spring onions.

Luckily the onion leaves were soft. But they smelt horribly. Harlequin in particular was furious.

'It's the very last time,' he shouted, 'that we shall engage you on any of our expeditions!'

'Engage!' said the wagon. 'Engage! That's good!' And he rumbled back to the house, squeaking all the way, 'Engage!'

'I suppose really we should have paid him something on account,' said Virginia May. 'But we never seem to have any money!'

The Money-Pig kept quiet, which was rather mean of him, for everyone knew he had all the money there was.

Bulka had fallen on his nose in the onion bed, which was really fortunate, for he had just opened his mouth to cry when the wagon tipped over, but, lying face downward on the soft earth, he couldn't do it. Now he picked himself up and repeated 'Hurrah!' instead.

A little way off, by the edge of the potato patch, they could see the big stone.

CHAPTER 3

How Poor Cecco lost his tail

IT was a very large stone – larger even than Bulka had thought. It looked as if it had lain there for a very long time; almost as if it had always been there, and the potato patch and the garden and even the house itself had just grown up around it. There might very well be treasure there; it might even be a magic stone, by the look of it.

'The first thing to do,' said Poor Cecco, 'is to measure off the ground.'

He began at once to measure it off in paces, five times his own length, counting the tail, and that brought him half-way down one of the furrows of the potato patch. There he found a little twig and stuck it up in the earth to mark the spot.

'That's five lengths,' he explained, 'and now if we measure five lengths from here again, in a straight line, it brings us back to the stone, and that shows exactly where we've got to dig.'

The others stood and watched him in admiration. It was all so perfectly simple and came out just right, only the Easter Chicken said:

'I don't see why you need measure just to get back to where you started from.'

'You've got to measure,' said Poor Cecco hastily, for he did not want them to start asking questions. 'It's got to be done like that, or it won't come out properly.'

'Do you mean the treasure won't come out?' asked the Easter Chicken.

But Poor Cecco put him back in the Wooden Engine and told him to keep quiet.

'I wish I hadn't come,' said the Easter Chicken, snuggling down inside the Engine. 'I'm sure it's going to be boring. Wake me up when you find the treasure,' he called out aloud.

Tubby and Bulka began to dig, taking turns with the spade, while Poor Cecco dug with his paws. Showers of earth flew over his back; soon there was quite a hole. It was exciting work, but the dolls grew tired of looking on; they wanted to see the treasure at once, and that was not possible. So they dragged Ida over to a more comfortable spot and sat down on her to gossip.

'Don't you think Harlequin is handsome?' asked Gladys. 'I find there is something so distinguished about him.'

'He is certainly good-looking,' said Virginia May, 'but even you must admit that he has very little conversation. I never hear him say anything but 'Hey Presto,' and that is bound to become monotonous after a time, even when you are married to a person.'

'I don't agree with you,' said Gladys. 'It is perhaps true that he seemed more intelligent before we were married, but that was probably due to shyness. He is extremely elegant, and after all what more can you want?'

'Domestic life is boring,' said Virginia May, 'and what's more, it makes people stupid and conceited. I intend to keep my independence.' And she made a movement to smooth out her skirts, but remembering that tonight she had none, sat with her hands folded stiffly on her lap, staring out at the potato patch.

'She is jealous,' thought Gladys. 'That is because she has no wedding dress, but what can I do? These things are arranged for one by fate.'

Ida sighed. Romantic by nature, she was doomed to spend her life listening to other people's confidences. No one ever thought of falling in love with her, and yet she had all the qualifications for an ideal wife.

Anna now was different. Anna held her head high. She stood now in the moonlight, serene on her little green meadow, her two glass eyes, set almost on the top of her woolly head, staring of necessity straight up into the sky. It gave her a rather stupid expression, but the lion did not notice that. He thought she was beautiful. He thought, in fact, she was the most beautiful person in the world.

'I adore you!' he said to her now for the hundredth time. 'Leave this barren country and fly with me to the jungle.'

'I don't think I should like the jungle,' said Anna. 'Everyone tells me it is full of snakes. I could never feel at home there.'

'How can you tell until you have tried?' objected the Lion. 'The jungle is a wonderful place. There is a green twilight within it, monkeys swing from branch to branch. There the birds have a thousand voices and the flowers are lovelier than the fairest dream. Fly with me, beautiful Anna, and we will be king and queen of the jungle for ever!'

'Would I really be queen?' Anna asked, for that interested her.

'You shall be queen of the whole forest,' said the Lion. 'A thousand slaves shall do your bidding and you shall wear garlands of flowers round your neck.'

"I adore you!"

'I cannot abandon my meadow,' said Anna primly. 'I have made a vow never to leave it.'

'Oh, of course,' retorted the Lion, really losing his temper this time, 'if you mean to spend all your life attached to a miserable bit of painted board, then there's no use arguing with you!'

And he turned his back on her in a great huff and went off to see how the treasure was getting on. Anna felt that she had pushed matters a little too far. She had no intention of settling down in the jungle, which she pictured as an overgrown bean-patch, but she liked to hear the Lion talk about it; he put everything in such a poetic light that it really sounded quite attractive. She wandered off now among the potatoes, hoping that the lion would change his mind and follow her, as he had done many times before, but he didn't. Anna was too proud to call him, so she blundered on and on, feeling that her evening was completely spoiled, and presently got lost among the potato vines for her pains, which served her right.

Meanwhile, quite a large hole had been dug under the stone, but there was so far nothing to show. Bulka's paws were blistered from digging; he was all for giving up the job and trying somewhere else, but the Money-Pig would not hear of this. The mere thought of treasure excited him, and as his legs were too short for him to dig himself he felt quite safe in giving orders to the others.

'Remember,' he kept shouting, 'I am the guardian of this treasure. I order you to keep on digging till you find it.'

'In Tubbyland,' Tubby began in her squeaky voice, 'whenever there is treasure it's *always* buried under big stones, and there's heaps and heaps of it, and whoever finds it it belongs to all of them, and as soon as ever you start digging—'

'I'm *sick* of hearing about Tubbyland,' said Bulka, sucking his paws that had begun to smart. 'I wish Tubbyland had never been invented!'

'Then if you say that,' said Tubby indignantly, 'it's just the same as saying you wish *I* had never been invented!'

'I do!' cried Bulka. 'I do wish you'd never been invented, so Hinksman!'

'Oh! Oh!' shrieked Tubby. 'Bulka's being unkind to me!'

Poor Cecco had to stop digging.

'Can't you two keep from quarrelling for one evening!' he exclaimed.

'Well, Tubby is so ucky!' said Bulka sulkily.

Now 'ucky' is the very horridest word you can use about anybody – you can tell from the sound how horrid it is – and things were likely to have gone very badly had not Harlequin suddenly had an idea. This did not happen to him often; up to the present he had contented himself with dancing about and saying 'Hey Presto' while the others worked, which did not assist matters much, but he felt now that this idea was too good to be wasted.

'Instead of digging the earth from under the stone,' he suggested, 'why don't we lift the stone off the treasure?'

Poor Cecco scratched his head. 'That's not a bad idea!'

'It's what I told you all along,' put in the Money-Pig, 'only no one listens to me!'

How to do it was the question. The stone was far too heavy to lift. All of them pushing together could not budge it an inch. 'We must lever,' said the Money-Pig. And then it was that Poor Cecco had his really bad inspiration. It all came out of trying to be too helpful.

'If I put my tail under it,' he said, 'we can use that for a lever and tilt it up.'

'Hey Presto,' cried Harlequin, striking an attitude.

Poor Cecco's tail was of wood, like all the rest of him, but it was a fine strong tail, and in those days quite long. It was an easy job to poke the tip of it under the stone. Really it looked as if it would make a wonderful lever, and Poor Cecco himself was quite excited. 'Now, all take hold of it together,' he cried, 'and when I say "ready" you must push as hard as you can!'

And he took a long breath and planted all his four feet very firmly and said 'Ready!'

What really did happen? No one knew. But at the moment they all crowded together, holding on to his tail, and Poor Cecco took his long breath, and everyone pushed, instead of the stone rolling over as they expected there was a dreadful crack, and Poor Cecco's lovely wooden tail snapped right in half!

That was a terrible moment! There was half of Poor Cecco's tail broke off under the stone, and what was worse, they couldn't pull it out again. Not that it would have been much use to him if they had. Tubby gave a piercing shriek, Harlequin turned very pale and tottered as he stood, the dolls hid their faces, and as for Bulka, he burst out crying louder and more like a five-finger exercise than ever before, and no one had the heart to stop him. They could only put their fingers in their ears and shake their heads and stamp.

'Indeed it doesn't hurt,' Poor Cecco was saying. 'Bulka, dear Bulka, I'll buy a new tail tomorrow if you'll stop crying!'

But Bulka refused to be comforted. His weeping swelled out on the breeze, loud and strong. All over the garden one could hear him, and all the potato bugs came running, wakened out of sleep, to know what the matter was. To Anna, however, lost among the potato vines and very miserable, it was a positive blessing. She lifted her head, stopped snivelling, and lumbered back, led by the sound, to where the others were gathered.

'What has happened?' she began. 'Have you found the treasure? Why is Bulka crying?'

'Poor Cecco has lost his tail!'

Then Anna had to cry too.

'Hoo – Hoo –' they all lamented. 'Poor Cecco has lost his tail!'

'Where did he lose it?' asked the potato bugs, who after all are practical people.

'He broke it off. Hoo – Hooo!'

'Then why did you say he lost it?' returned the eldest potato bug, slightly annoyed. 'Lost is one thing, broken another. We can't do anything about that!' And the potato bugs all humped their backs and crawled back to bed again.

Now there must be an ambulance, and it was no use shouting for the express wagon. He had been sound asleep again these two hours past. So they turned the Easter Chicken out of the wooden Engine and put Poor Cecco in that. His legs hung over the side; it wasn't very comfortable, but it was the best they could manage. Harlequin was to be the doctor. He was the tallest and could look quite wise so long as he didn't open his mouth, and there was no need for that. Tubby and Virginia May would be hospital nurses and wear a red cross on their arm. They arranged it all, walking on either side the Engine to keep Poor Cecco from falling out. It was almost as exciting as if they had found the treasure, and they had the added satisfaction of doing good to someone at the same time.

So they walked home, Anna pulling the engine, and Tubby and Virginia on either side, and whenever they met anyone on the road they put their handkerchiefs to their eyes and said: 'Poor Cecco has lost his tail!'

As for Poor Cecco, he got a ride home anyway, and when they reached the toy-cupboard they put him to bed in the dolls' cradle and there he slept peacefully and Bulka sat by his side all night.

CHAPTER 4

Bulka and Poor Cecco decide to see the world

IN the morning when Poor Cecco woke he had forgotten all about his tail. But he remembered it as soon as he jumped out of bed and stood up. It felt so funny without it. There was nothing to wag but a little stump that went to and fro very fast, like a clock with the pendulum taken off.

'That's not so bad!' thought Poor Cecco, and skipped over to look at himself in the glass. 'Half a tail is better than no tail. Besides, many of the best people wear it that way!'

It was quite early, but there was already light in the room. Long strips of sunlight came in under the drawn window-shade. All the toys were asleep. They were very tired from staying up so late the night before.

'Now is the time to go for a walk!' said Poor Cecco, and he called to Bulka very softly so as not to waken the others.

Bulka had fallen asleep with his nose on the edge of the doll's cradle. But he woke up at once with a jump, rubbing his eyes.

'We are going for a walk!' said Poor Cecco.

'But how about your tail?' Bulka asked.

'My tail can very well look after itself,' Poor Cecco replied. 'Besides, if we stay here the others will want to play at hospital, and that I can't stand. Do you remember the last time Tubby had measles and Virginia pinned the bedclothes on her to keep them tidy?'

Of course Bulka remembered. The pin had gone right into Tubby's middle, and Virginia was quite annoyed because she had to pull it out again.

'This time,' Poor Cecco said, 'we'll give them something that won't matter, to practise on!'

So he fetched a stick of firewood from the box in the kitchen. They put it in the doll's cradle and pulled the covers up close, and it looked quite like a real wooden person lying there.

No one was astir in the house. Outside on the doorstep Murrum, returned from his wanderings, was sniffing round the milk-bottles. He gave Poor Cecco a surly look.

'Now we know where the milk goes!' jeered Poor Cecco.

But he had to dodge quickly down the steps and round the rain-water butt. Lucky for him that Murrum was feeling stiff and drowsy!

The road stretched out, like a great ribbon reaching to the ends of the world. The sun shone down, and all the grass blades had gleaming tips. It was a fine day to set out for adventures. Presently a man overtook them, driving a wagon piled high with hay.

'Do you want a lift?' he cried. 'It's lucky to meet one wooden leg, so four must be better still! Climb up on my wagon, and I'll take you into the town.'

Bulka and Poor Cecco climbed up. The countryman cracked his whip, and away they went down the road. This was better than the express wagon! The hay was as soft and springy as a feather bed. But one must take care not to fall off, and that wasn't so easy; the wagon pitched and swayed like a ship at sea, and Poor Cecco had to cling tight with all his paws. As for Bulka, he just lay and bounced.

That was a fine way to ride into town, with all the bells on the harness jingling and the wagon wheels a creak and the driver snapping his whip. The only trouble was that Bulka, long before they passed the last milestone, began to feel seasick.

The driver pulled up his horses just past the bridge at the beginning of the town.

'Now I must put you down,' he said, 'for I have to drive on to the dealer and sell my hay. So good-bye, and thank you for your company!'

And being a nice man, he reached out his arm and helped them to the ground.

By the end of the bridge a blind man was sitting, with his back against the wall, dozing in the sunshine. Beside him sat a little black dog, keeping watch over a tin can that was placed there for pennies. There were only three pennies in it as yet, for it was still early and not many people had passed over the bridge. The blind man was very old, with a long white beard, and the little black dog was old too, and turning grey about the whiskers. But he was a pleasant-looking dog, and Poor Cecco, being a stranger in the town, thought it well to be polite to everyone. So he said:

'It's a fine morning!'

'It is a fine morning,' returned the little black dog without turning his head, 'and fine enough for you who can run about and enjoy it! Not that I grudge it you, but it's small pleasure to sit here day in and day out, and never a chance to stretch my legs a bit and see what's going on in the world. No, we who have to work don't get much fun out of life, and that's the truth!'

'Why do you have to sit there all day?' asked Poor Cecco. 'Don't you ever take a holiday?'

'And who'd look after my old man here, if I went gadding about?' said the little dog. 'I'm in charge of him, and he can't be left to himself. He's a good sort, so far as that goes, and I'm quite fond of him, but I don't mind saying I'd like a change now and again. I fetch him out every morning and I take him home at night, and between whiles I must sit here and look after the pennies.'

Poor Cecco peered into the tiny cup.

'I should think the pennies could very well look after themselves,' he said.

'That shows how much you know about it,' returned the little dog. 'It's easy to tell you're from the country, even if I hadn't seen you ride up on the hay wagon! Still, I like the look of you, and I can't say that of everyone.'

'Suppose I take your place for a while?' said Poor Cecco, who was anxious to be friendly. 'I'll sit here and watch the pennies, and give you a chance to walk about a bit and see the town.'

The little dog stared at him.

'That's an idea worth thinking about,' he said. 'But how can I tell you'll look after the business properly? I can't have my old man robbed by anyone who may come along.'

'Leave that to me,' said Poor Cecco. 'As for Bulka here, he'll sit by and help me. Only take your head out of the collar and let me get mine in.'

So the little dog pulled his head out of the collar, very carefully, so as not to waken the old man, and Poor Cecco slipped his head through instead. The collar was far too big, but he managed to prop it up somehow, and there he sat on the pavement, with the tin cup at his feet.

'That's a neighbourly act,' said the little dog. 'I will do as much for you, some day. Now look pleasant, and above all, don't forget to wag your tail for a penny! It pleases the people and draws custom.'

And he strolled off down the road, very pleased with himself, stretching his legs and sniffing at all the corners like any fine gentlemanly dog of leisure.

The first passer-by paid no attention at all, but strode by in a great hurry without even looking their way. The second paused and stared, but just as Poor Cecco was getting his half tail ready to wag, he too passed on. But the third one stopped long enough to put his hand in his pocket and drop a penny into the tin cup, and thump went Poor Cecco's tail on the pavement, just as the little black dog had told him. He couldn't wag it sideways, for it wasn't made that way, but he lifted it up and let it drop – bang – just like a door-knocker, and that did quite as well.

'That's a fine sort of dog you've got,' said the stranger, who had the look of a countryman.

The blind man aroused, and nodded his head.

'He's a good enough dog,' he said.

'And he won't eat you out of house and home either, I'll be bound,' said the man.

'He eats what he can get,' returned the blind man, 'but we must all do that.'

'That's the sort of dog I wouldn't mind keeping myself,' said the countryman. 'I suppose you wouldn't be wanting to sell him?'

'No, I wouldn't sell him,' said the blind man. 'We've been friends too long, and you don't find a dog like him every day.'

Poor Cecco thought the little black dog might well be pleased to hear that, for of course the blind man couldn't know that they had changed places. Other passers-by stopped, seeing the countryman standing there, and they too had pennies to drop in the cup. Soon there was quite a crowd. No one before had ever seen a wooden dog that wagged

its tail; it was as good as going to the circus, and the pennies rattled down. One man put as many as three. And when they grew tired of staring and passed on others came forward to take their places. Poor Cecco's tail went thump – thump – on the pavement; he could scarcely keep count any more and soon the cup was overflowing. Those who had no more pennies put in dimes and nickels. Business was certainly flourishing.

The old blind man had never known such a good morning before.

'It must be because the sun is shining,' he said to himself as he heard the coins clinking in the cup. 'Everyone is in a good humour. Yes, it must certainly be a very sunny day!'

In the middle of it all the little black dog came strolling back. There was such a crowd that he had to push his way between the people's legs.

'You've surely done well!' he said. 'I give credit where credit's due, and I'm sorry I called you a hayseed. I can see now you've got a head for affairs, and if you like to stay here and go into partnership with me and my old man we'll give you a share in the business and a corner to sleep in at night.'

But that didn't suit Poor Cecco at all. He was tired of sitting still by now, and his tail was quite stiff and painful from so much thumping. He was glad enough to slip his head out of the collar and let the little dog take his place again.

'Business is all very well,' he said, 'but my friend and I came out to see the world, and I've only seen part of it as yet. Still I've learned now how money can be made, and that's always useful if you happen to want it.' And he thanked him kindly and went on his way, though not before the little dog had insisted on Poor Cecco accepting four pennies, three for himself and one over for his friend.

'Bulka will be pleased with this!' thought Poor Cecco.

But when he turned round to look for Bulka, Bulka wasn't there!

CHAPTER 5

Bulka gets into trouble

WHERE was Bulka?

When Poor Cecco changed places with the little black dog, and sat down on the pavement to wait for pennies, Bulka soon got very bored with sitting there beside him, and nothing at all to do. So bye-and-bye he got up, quietly, without saying a word, and strolled off along the sidewalk to see what there was to be seen.

The bridge, like a great many other bridges, had water flowing beneath it. And a few steps farther on, not far from where the old man sat, a little path ran down a steep bank from the sidewalk to the water's edge.

Now Bulka loved water. He had often thought that he would like to be a sailor, in spite of the fact that the least rocking made him seasick. And he had never seen so much water as this before. In fact, all the water he had seen, up to now, had been in tubs and pails, or else in puddles on the garden path after a shower, and these were shallow and muddy, and always dried up just when the sun shone out and you didn't want them to. But here was water, plenty of it, flowing along as freely as if there were no end to it all, as indeed there wasn't, and as soon as Bulka caught sight of it he became very excited.

'Someone,' he thought, 'has left the spigot running!' And he began at once to slide down the little path as fast as he could go, on his behind legs.

In the pool under the bridge a number of ducks were swimming about; big ducks and middle-size ducks, and some little furry baby ducks, with flat yellow feet and eyes like drops of ink. They swam about in circles, dabbling under the water with their bills, while a little way off, all by himself, an old drake with green feathers was asleep on the water, with his head tucked under his wing.

At first the ducks took no notice of Bulka, and for a long time he amused himself by poking about on the shore by the water's edge, getting his feet very muddy, and looking under all the stones. For if treasure really grew under stones, as Poor Cecco had said, here might be a very good place to find it. But nothing grew under these stones except fat pink worms, and one horrid black thing with pincers, which behaved very rudely and which Bulka did not like the look of at all.

So after a time he gave up the hunt, as the things he found under the stones seemed to be getting worse and worse, and instead he sat down on a tuft of grass to watch the ducks.

They were having a wonderful time, dabbling here and poking there, and every little while one of them would stand right on his head in the water, with only his tail sticking out and his yellow feet paddling away at a great rate; it was amazing how they did it, and it looked so easy! Even the baby ducks could do it, as cleverly as their elders.

It would be a fine thing to be a duck, Bulka thought, and stand on one's head in the water, and almost before he knew it he was trying to do the same thing on shore. But it wasn't so simple as it looked, perhaps because there was no water to keep him up, and the best he could do was to turn a sort of somersault and fall back each time on the mud.

'Here, what are you trying to do?' called the ducks. 'You won't catch any worms that way!'

'I'm not looking for worms,' said Bulka, feeling suddenly shy when he found they were all watching him, but keeping up his somersaults none the less, just to show them that he didn't care. 'I don't like worms!'

'Don't like worms?' cried the biggest duck, and all the little ones came crowding up at once to see this strange person who didn't like worms.

'Your head is too big,' said one of the younger ducks, after watching him for a moment attentively.

'Come out here,' called another, 'and we'll show you how to do it properly!'

'I don't need showing,' said Bulka.

'Well, *I* call that a silly performance!' remarked the big duck after a while, and shaking her feathers she swam off to look for frogs across the stream. But the younger ones all stayed round, watching.

'Come out into the water!' they cried. And the smallest and most impudent duckling of all called out suddenly: 'I believe he's afraid!'

'I'm not afraid!' returned Bulka, very red in the face, but still going on with his somersaults.

'If you aren't afraid why don't you come out?' asked the ducks. 'Coward!'

This was more than Bulka could stand. He couldn't endure being called a coward, so he took a flying jump then and there and landed right in the water where the ducks were paddling about. The water wasn't very deep, but it was quite cold, and tasted very slimy and muddy; a great deal of it went up Bulka's nose and down his throat, for he had forgotten to keep his mouth shut when he jumped, and as soon as he poked his head above water to breathe one of the ducklings would catch him by his long ears and pull him under again. 'Down you go!' they shouted. 'Now stick your feet in the air!'

It was a fine game for them, but poor Bulka, tangled up in the pondweed with his head under water, was very close to being drowned, and drowned he would surely have been had not Poor Cecco, who at that very moment was looking about for him on the bridge, heard one smothered squeal and poked his head hastily through the parapet.

'There's Bulka in trouble again!' he exclaimed, and came galloping – clop – clop – down the little path to the stream. In a moment he was out among the ducks and had dragged Bulka away from them, not an instant too soon, and even then it was a hard tussle, for one of the ducklings had hold of Bulka firmly by the ear and wouldn't let go. But Poor Cecco was a good swimmer, being made of wood; he dealt blows about him right and left with his feet, and moreover it was no good trying to bite him, he was far too hard, and one of the ducks who did try it had toothache for a week after. So they let Bulka go, and Poor Cecco towed him back to shore and set him up in the sunshine to dry. He was covered with slime and pondweed, one ear had come unsewn in the tussle, and altogether he looked a miserable object, but he was glad enough to be back on dry land. And I'm ashamed to say that the first thing he did, when he had his breath back and had got rid of the water he swallowed, was to turn round and make a very rude and ugly face at the ducklings, who only laughed at him for his pains.

While Bulka sat there drying off, and picking the pondweed out of his ears, Poor Cecco set about looking for a boat. He wandered up and down the shore, and at last discovered a piece of plank big enough to hold the two of them safely, and with a hole at one end in which he stuck a branch of willow, with the green leaves still on it, for a mast. It looked quite elegant, and when he had dragged it down to the water and launched it there was a fine raft in which they could set out to explore the stream.

The mast stood up bravely, the green leaves shaking in the breeze just like a real sail; Poor Cecco and Bulka took their places in the stern, and off they went, gliding easily through the water. To be sure there was no rudder, but Poor Cecco had already thought of that. He had a piece of shingle in his paws for an oar, and this he dipped first on one side and then on the other, and so managed to keep their vessel on its course.

They could not make up their minds whether to go upstream or down, but this was soon decided for them; there was no choice but to follow the current, and this took them first of all under the bridge. They drifted past the ducks, who stopped scratching their heads with their toes to stare at them, very politely now they saw that Bulka was owner of a real ship and not to be taken liberties with any more. To be sure the most impudent duckling did swim after them, opening his bill, but Poor Cecco gave him a rap with the oar and very soon sent him about his business.

It was quite dark under the bridge; green moss hung from the stones and water dripped down on them from the arched roof. It was like entering a long dark tunnel; all sorts of horrible things might be lurking there. No sooner had they left daylight than a terrible noise began. It was only a wagon rumbling over the bridge above them, but Bulka thought it was a real storm and began to get frightened. It shook and thundered as if the whole bridge were going to tumble on their heads and little stones and lumps of earth splashed in the water about them.

'We must turn back!' cried Bulka. But this they could not do; all Poor Cecco could manage was to keep as straight a course as possible in spite of the tumult, and very soon they shot out once more into the sunlight and open sky.

Everything looked very dazzling after the twilight under the bridge; it was like coming out into a new world. Great dragonflies swooped to and fro, and there were red and white and yellow flowers blooming along the green meadow-banks. On one of the flat bronze leaves with turned-up edges like a tea-tray, that floated on the stream, a frog sat. He was banded green and yellow, with gold eyes, and as the boat drew near he gave a loud mournful cry and dived into the water. A spotted mud turtle lay sunning himself on a log; he did not move, but watched them with black unwinking eyes as they drifted past, his wrinkled neck half drawn within his shell and his horny toes outstretched. Cows were grazing in the meadows on either side, and a little white dog who was out chasing water-rats, ran beside the boat for a long time on the riverbank, barking.

'Ah, if we only had some chocolate cake and peanut candy!' thought Bulka.

But neither of them had thought to bring food, which is a great mistake on a voyage, for there were no shops along the riverbank, only grass and green rushes.

Still it was very pleasant drifting along, following the twists and turns of the stream. In some places the current ran very strongly, and Poor Cecco had to bend hard on the oar to keep the vessel from running ashore. Once they were caught in an eddy and very nearly upset. Certainly one needed to be a good navigator.

'We shall soon be on the other side of the world, at this rate,' thought Bulka, and he asked Poor Cecco: 'Do all the rivers go to the same place?'

'They all flow into the sea,' replied Poor Cecco, who had learned that much from an old geography book.

'Where does all the water come from?' asked Bulka.

But that Poor Cecco did not know, so he changed the subject. 'Let's talk about roads instead,' he said.

'Do rivers go faster or do roads go faster?' Bulka wanted to know.

Poor Cecco needed to think. 'The roads go faster,' he said at last. 'There is only one road and it goes all over the world and when it reaches the sea it has to turn round and come back again, and that

makes it twice as long and so it has to go faster than the rivers to catch up.'

'What happens,' said Bulka, 'if they both get there the same time?'

'Then they have to change places and start all over again.'

'I'd rather be the river,' said Bulka. He lay on his back, staring up at the sky with his round eyes. The sky was very blue, with little white clouds racing across it like flocks of sheep. The water made a pleasant drowsy ripple against the boat, and Bulka began to get sleepy. His bath too had tired him out, and before he knew it he was snoring aloud.

'That's not such a bad idea either!' thought Poor Cecco. And he steered the boat into a little bay, right under the shade of some huge burdock leaves, and folded his legs under him and went to sleep beside Bulka on the deck.

CHAPTER 6

The storm

THEY must have slept quite a long time, for when they woke up it was nearly dusk. There was a storm coming on; big drops were already pattering on the burdock leaves, and it was one of these, tumbling straight on his nose, that roused Poor Cecco from slumber He sat up, looked about him, and was just in time to push the boat farther under shelter when the storm broke.

It was raining now in good earnest. The wind blew strongly and black jagged clouds were racing across the sky. And at once the little rainpeople appeared everywhere on the surface of the water, bobbing up and down and shouting. Bulka began to whimper and crept as close to Poor Cecco as he could. Soon the boat was rocking to and fro. The burdock leaves bent beneath the weight of moisture; little rivulets trickled down their broad stems. Before long the two friends were drenched through and through.

They were so wet that the water ran out through their heels, and to make matters worse the stream itself, swollen with the rain, began to rise; great waves swept down it with a rushing sound, awful things were happening out there in the darkness and at any moment they felt the vessel might be torn from its moorings and carried away on the flood.

'We must jump!' cried Poor Cecco, and seizing Bulka by the paw he leapt ashore. Only just in time, for at that very moment the raft began to sink beneath their feet and was lost.

Bulka, who had never before been out in a storm at night, was afraid of the noise and darkness, and sobbed bitterly. To him it seemed that the whole world was sliding into the river, and they were about to perish miserably, in the wet and the cold. He lifted up his voice and wept, while Poor Cecco, still clutching his paw, dragged him up the bank to a place of safety.

Here, pressed close against a decaying tree-stump, they waited shivering until the worst of the storm had abated. Somewhere they must seek warmth and shelter, but where?

'You stay here,' said Poor Cecco, 'while I go out and see what can be done.'

But Bulka would not hear of this; he was far too frightened and miserable. So paw in paw the two ventured out together into the unknown darkness.

The earth was sticky and muddy; it clung in lumps to their feet, and there were deep sloshy puddles everywhere. The weeds grew high above their heads, a dense forest. It was impossible to see one's way. The rain was still falling steadily.

Poor Cecco saw something shining in the darkness and ran towards it. 'There's a light!' he cried.

But it was only a tin can, battered, and shining in the wet. Near it lay an old boot. That was no help either, for it was soaked through and gaping at the toe. In any case there was not room for them both to creep inside.

'If only there were a box,' thought Poor Cecco, 'we could crawl into that and be sheltered till the morning.' But it is always the way with boxes, that however many there may be in the world one is never to be found when you most need it.

There was nothing to do but keep on, but presently they found a path at least. It was not much of a path, but fairly plain to trace between the tall weeds, and it must surely lead somewhere, for that is what paths are for. And it did lead them presently, and after a very long time, to a tumbledown wooden fence.

Poor Cecco stood and sniffed.

'It smells like a house,' he said at last. 'Yes, it certainly smells like a house!' And he squeezed himself through the wooden palings and dragged Bulka after him.

Here perhaps was the end of their troubles. A house it might be, but the question was, what sort of people lived in it, and that wasn't easy to tell from the outside, especially after dark. But while they stood there shivering, and wondering whether they should go to the door and knock, there was a rustling among the bushes, and someone poked his nose out.

Sure enough, of all unexpected things, it was the little black dog who took care of the blind man on the bridge!

'Well, here's a fine finish to your sight-seeing!' he exclaimed. 'Didn't I tell you you'd do better to stay with me? It's a good thing I was listening at the door, or you might have stayed here till morning. But my cottage is not far off, and there's still a bit of fire to warm yourselves by!'

'Do you live here?' cried Poor Cecco and Bulka both at once.

'Indeed I don't,' returned the little dog. 'There's a nasty old woman lives here, and she'd soon send you chasing with a broom if you go near her door after dusk! But follow me, and I'll take you where you'll be warm and dry.'

So they squeezed through the palings again, the little black dog leading the way, and followed him – trot – trot – along the path, till he turned in by a clump of currant bushes, and there was the door of his cottage, with a fine beam of light shining out through the crack underneath.

The little dog barked twice, and the blind man let him in. To be sure he grumbled, but that was at the little black dog, because he had been obliged to open the door for him twice already that evening, and each time the rain beat in, and as he rightly explained, that sort of thing was bad for anyone's rheumatism.

'He's a rare grumbler,' said the little dog, 'but don't you mind him. He means nothing by it, and he'll be asleep again in two minutes. And now make yourselves at home!'

The blind man's cottage had only one room, but it was warm and comfortable. The stove burned cheerfully, there was a bed in one corner where the blind man slept and another under the table for the little dog. On the floor stood a saucer of bread-and-milk, left over from the little dog's own supper, which he said they might finish up and welcome; as for himself, he had all he wanted.

While they were sitting round the stove, getting thoroughly warm and dry, the old blind man took his fiddle down from the wall and began to play. It was wonderful how he drew the bow across the strings, and at once the music came out, capital tunes, one after another, that made one long to get up and dance. The little dog sat still, blinking; he had heard these tunes many times before and took no great stock in them, he said, one air was just like another to him. The blind man's head nodded as he played, and his foot tapped on the boards. Presently Poor Cecco could stand it no longer. He jumped up, and seizing Bulka round the waist began to whirl him about the floor. It was a pity the little dog didn't dance too. If Virginia May and Tubby had been there, what a wonderful time they would have had! It seemed too bad that they should miss this, when Tubby so dearly loved dancing, and the only music they could get at home was the broken musical-box, that would only play three notes and then stop.

The blind man smiled; with his sightless eyes he was seeing again the old farmhouse kitchens in the country, where he had been such a fine dancer in his youth, and all the girls were proud to stand up beside him. But presently his head drooped; his foot ceased to tap on

... getting thoroughly warm and dry.

the floor and he rose yawning and hung his fiddle up on the wall again. He was old and sleepy, and he wanted to smoke another pipe before he went to bed.

And now there was a rap at the door, and the little dog pulled back the latch. It was Mrs Greypuss, who lived next door but one. She had tucked her babies in bed and come across in the rain to learn what the festivity was about.

'You're having a good time here,' she said. 'I thought I'd step over a minute and join you, seeing the storm is nearly over!'

So she sat down beside Bulka and Poor Cecco, who were still out of breath from dancing, and they chatted together while the fire died down in the stove and the old man nodded off to sleep, his pipe between his fingers; and presently Mrs Greypuss, who could never sit idle for long, took a needle and thread from the useful little pocket that all cats wear in their ears, and sewed Bulka up where his stitches had come undone, so that he was all strong and ready for the morrow.

'For who knows?' she said, 'what further adventures you two are going to meet!'

CHAPTER 7

Jensina

THEY had passed such a pleasant evening, once the storm was over, that it seemed a pity to say good-bye to the little dog again in the morning, and watch him trot off, leading his old man securely on a string, along the path to the town. He walked very jauntily, a few steps ahead of the blind man and a little faster, so that every now and then he had to pause and turn his head back, as if to say: 'How slow you are this morning! We shall never get to the bridge and start business at this rate!'

Poor Cecco and Bulka waited long enough to wave their paws at him at the bend of the road; then they turned their face towards the open field. But first they stopped to say good morning to Mrs Greypuss, who sat washing her face on the doorstep, with her three little kittens playing near her. The-old-woman-with-the-broom they did not see, but they were careful not to go too near her house, from which they could hear a great sound of sweeping and clattering of saucepans.

The cottages where the little black dog and Mrs Greypuss and the-old-woman-with-the-broom lived stood on the edge of a big and very untidy field. The field was untidy because, being close to the road, and belonging to no one in particular, the dustmen had used it to dump all the ashes and tin cans and broken crockery that no one wanted to have about. But the weeds grew very tall and thick, to hide the untidiness that the dustmen made, and however fast the dustmen brought their loads of rubbish the weeds always managed to grow a little faster, so on the whole the field was not nearly as bad-looking as it might have been.

And certainly all sorts of curious and useful things lay there, for anyone who had time to look about – bits of old automobiles, and lamp-chimneys and oil-stoves, and cracked china plates with most beautiful patterns on them, and here and there a perfectly good boot or coffeepot – and all these things, having been thoroughly washed by the night's rain, were displayed among the fresh green weeds like goods in a huge shop-window. Bulka in particular, never having seen such attractive objects going to waste before, was continually wanting to stop and pick something up, and as the things he wanted were nearly all too big for him to carry, Poor Cecco had a hard time dragging him past them by the paw. And every moment Bulka kept exclaiming: 'I'm sure Tubby would like that!' or, 'Can't we take this home to Gladys?'

Presently, seated beside one of the largest ash-heaps, they met a little wooden doll. She was tidily dressed in a check gingham apron, which she had made herself, with a pink mallow-blossom on her head, and was so pleased to see visitors that she jumped up at once when she saw them coming and clapped her hands.

Her name, she told them, was Jensina, and she had been living alone on this ash-heap for weeks and weeks and weeks. She was an industrious little person, one could see at once, and had not wasted her time, for when she led them presently round the side of the ash-heap there stood a cosy little house which she had built herself, out of an old soap-box, and of which she had every reason to be proud. She had spread a bit of carpet on the floor and made a sofa to sleep on, and pillows stuffed with thistledown, and she had hung the walls with scraps of wallpaper and fine pictures of tomatoes and peach-orchards, saved from old fruit cans. She had even a little kitchen, with plates and egg-cups and a real coffeepot, and all these things she had gathered one by one on the dump-heaps and brought home. Only the coffeepot being too large, had to stand outside, but it looked very well there, and gave an air of hospitality to the place.

While they sat on the sofa at her invitation, and breakfasted on some canned salmon and graham cracker which she had very luckily brought home just before the storm yesterday, the wooden doll told them her story.

'From the earliest time I can remember,' she said, 'I lived with a family of travelling gypsies. They were kindly, hard-working people, and I spent very happy days in their company. By day we travelled the roads in a cart drawn by an old white horse, and while the women and children worked at making brooms and baskets which they sold by the way, the men did odd jobs of tinkering, mending saucepans and pails for the farmers' wives at different houses where we stopped, and in that way I saw a great deal of the country, besides learning much gypsy lore, and picking up several trades that are useful to know. At night, when the horse was taken from the wagon and turned out to graze, supper was cooked at an open fire by the roadside, and after that the family would gather round and sing songs and tell old stories, and though there might be little to eat everyone was gay and happy.

'In winter, when the cold weather set in, they joined a circus in one of the small towns, and found employment there, till the summer came round once more. I had wonderful dresses in those days, for my gypsy child would sew them out of scraps of silk and lace from the circus-riders' costumes, that the old wardrobe women gave her to play with. It was a finc life with the circus, but I liked still better the rides in the old wagon under the open sky, and the evenings round the fire at night.

'Yes, I was happy with my gypsies, and I should be with them now had not an accident happened.

'One day the little girl left me lying too near the step of the wagon, and when the horse started I was presently jolted out and dropped by the roadside. Though I called for help no one heard me. There I lay till a workman, passing by, picked me up and took me home to his children.

'They were kind children enough, but not so kind as my gypsy child; they could never love me so well, for they had other dolls of their own, and presently they gave me away. So I passed from hand to hand, each time faring a little worse, until the last family with whom I lived changed house. They did not trouble to take me with them, so I was thrown out here, with the rest of the household rubbish, on the ash-heap.

'Still, I don't complain, for I am used to freedom and independence; all that I learned with the gypsies has stood me in good stead, and as you see I have not wasted my time.'

'Indeed,' said Poor Cecco, looking about him, 'you have made a very comfortable house here.'

The wooden doll smiled, for to tell the truth she felt not a little proud of her house, and was glad of someone to show it off to.

'It isn't so bad,' she agreed, 'and I must say there is always a living to be picked up in a place like this, especially by one who has been taught to use his wits. I even thought of starting a store here, if only there were some customers. No, the only thing I have against it is the loneliness. Just think, you are the only visitors I have received in all this time, unless you may count the rats, who are really of another class – neighbourly, but rowdy in their habits and by no means to be trusted. In fact, they think nothing of dropping in here and helping themselves to whatever they choose, claiming that everything in the field belongs to them. I have thought many times of moving, if only for the sake of change. Besides, I come of a gypsy family, and that always makes it hard to stay in one place.'

'Why don't you join us?' asked Poor Cecco. 'We are out to see the world, and it would be pleasant to have another companion.'

And Bulka, who all this while had been silent, licking the last of the canned salmon from his paws, said at once: 'Yes, do!'

Jensina agreed – she was really tired of living alone on the ash-heap – and being a person of action, at once set about packing up, with the help of Poor Cecco, those belongings which she especially treasured. These were a green glass scent bottle stopper, the half of a broken silver brooch, the top of a catsup bottle which made an excellent drinking-cup and one other small object wrapped in silver paper, which she would not show him. 'For this,' as she said, 'this is a secret which I dare not tell, even to you!'

To these Poor Cecco added his four pennies, and then, taking off her frock for greater freedom in walking, Jensina tied the things up in it, making a neat bundle which Poor Cecco willingly offered to carry.

Meantime, Bulka, who could not resist poking about the ash-heap, had found a damaged string of blue beads, brought to light by the heavy rain, which would make a marvellous present for Tubby. They were almost embedded in the earth; he seized one end of the string and was just giving it a strong tug when a great grey rat poked his head from among the weeds.

The rat, who looked very savage, began to twitch his nose and show his teeth, but Bulka clung to the beads manfully, although he was more than a little frightened. The rat came forward, sniffing the air, his whiskers twinkling, stretching out his body and leaving his hind feet behind him as long as possible, in the way rats do when they feel uncertain. Suddenly the string of beads came loose from the mud; Bulka fell back, uttering a loud howl, and at that very instant the rat opened his mouth to bite. In the flash of an eye, it seemed, there were rats all about him – grey rats, brown rats, black rats – all with long yellow teeth and snakelike tails.

Bulka, clutching his beads, set up a shriek for help, and immediately Poor Cecco and Jensina came scrambling over the crest of the ash-heap.

When she saw the rats Jensina for a second turned pale.

'See,' she exclaimed, 'they are blocking our way! They have been listening, they know that I am going to leave them and now they are sorry! Bark, Poor Cecco, bark! It is our only chance!'

And while Poor Cecco charged down the ash-heap, barking as he had never barked before, Jensina snatched pieces of cinder and crockery from the ground and flung them at the rats with all her strength – so desperately that she very nearly threw herself after them.

Even then the rats would not give way, until Jensina, seeing the fight was unequal, said: 'Well, there is only one thing to be done. We must take our chance!' And raising herself on tiptoe and waving her arms, she called out several words in rat language, which she had learned during her stay in the field.

The effect was instantaneous. The rats, with looks of amazement, horror and alarm, turned at once and rushed off through the weeds. In a second there was not one left in sight!

The battle was over, but the friends were in sore plight. Bulka had been bitten twice, Poor Cecco was hoarse from barking, and Jensina had slipped on the ash-heap and rolled from top to bottom, grazing herself severely.

'Horrid mean things!' she cried, rubbing her knees and picking up her bundle, which had come undone in the skirmish. 'They think they own everything here, and that no one has any rights but them. I'm glad I am going with you, for now nothing would induce me to stay here any longer!'

'At least,' said Poor Cecco, 'they have gone now, so we have nothing to fear.'

'They have gone for the moment,' Jensina said, 'but we must make haste, for I fear there is very little time to lose, and I shall be much mistaken if we have seen the last of them!'

Sawdust was oozing from Bulka's wound, but for once he didn't mind; he had the blue beads for Tubby and that was all he could think about for the moment. Jensina bound a dock-leaf over the bite, declaring that this was the best cure for injuries, and then, tightly holding paws, they made their escape as fast as they could over the ash-heap, not feeling really safe until they had reached the edge of the road.

CHAPTER 8

The pursuit

POOR Cecco wanted to take to the open country, but Jensina was all for the road. She was used to roads, she said, and felt at home on them.

'Are you afraid we can't defend you?' Poor Cecco asked.

'It isn't so much that,' said Jensina, pausing to brush the dust off her shoes, which, being painted directly on her feet, were extremely comfortable for walking. 'It isn't so much *that*, as that there's more life going on along the road. It seems years since I saw a wagon or an automobile, and if we are going to bury ourselves in the wilderness again I might as well have stayed on my ash-heap, where at least there was comfort!'

It was plain that the incident of the rats had upset her more than she would admit. So the others took no notice of her snippiness, but walked along on either side of her, affecting to admire the scenery.

There was very little passing certainly on this road. It was wide and bare and empty, and extremely hot, the sun by now being high above them, and not a cloud in the sky. Even the weeds along the roadside hung their heads. But along the edge of the road, down in the ditch, ran a trickle of water. Not enough to launch a boat on, but there was plenty to cool their feet, and very soon Poor Cecco and Bulka had hopped down and were walking along in it, splashing merrily. It looked so cool that Jensina had to follow their example. Besides, as Poor Cecco said, in this way the rats would be unable to trace their footsteps.

Jensina, like many another young lady, recovered her spirits as soon as she felt she was getting her own way; she sang snatches of songs and dances, and was altogether a most cheerful companion. Once in a while, on the road above them, an automobile passed with a noise like thunder and the blowing of trumpets, and whenever this happened Jensina scrambled hastily up the side of the ditch, her legs working like a pair of compasses, but she was always too late to see anything but a vanishing cloud of dust.

'I shall walk on the edge of the road!' she called finally. 'It is smoother up here, and one sees far more!'

So she walked along, tilting on her toes and turning her head from side to side as she went. But suddenly she came sliding in a great hurry down the side of the ditch again, very pale, her fingers on her lips.

'Sh-sh!' she whispered. 'The rats are following us! I knew they would!'

'Where?' cried Poor Cecco. 'Show me!'

Stealthily they all three climbed up the bank and peeped through the grasses. There, sure enough, coming at a steady pace along the road behind them, were two enormous rats. Even at that distance one could see their whiskers twitching and their eyes peering from side to side. At sight of them Bulka's bites, which he had nearly forgotten about, began to smart again.

'We'll keep quite still,' said Poor Cecco, 'and perhaps they will pass by and not see us.'

So they lay down, as flat as they could, among the grasses, scarcely daring to breathe. But the rats must have known they were there. For as soon as they came within a few feet of where the three friends were in hiding they stopped short, puffiing and blowing, and sat down in the road to consult.

'It's no use,' said Jensina, 'they must certainly have seen us. They are policemen rats.'

They were very fat rats, and elderly. They were hot and tired from coming so far along the dusty road. One of them, who was in quite a perspiration, began at once to mop his face and brush his whiskers, grumbling as he did so, and staring about him.

Jensina was watching them intently.

'I can't hear what they are saying,' she whispered, 'but at any rate they are not going to attack us now. The best thing is to go straight on, and pretend to take no notice of them.' And so saying, she rose to her feet, and humming a little tune, began to walk away. Bulka and Poor Cecco followed, looking back over their shoulders.

The two rats waited a little while. Then they too stood up, shook themselves, and resumed their steady trot.

'This is very mysterious,' said Poor Cecco to Bulka, 'and I begin to think that Jensina knows rather more about it than she is willing to tell us!'

Seeing, however, that the rats made no effort to overtake them, but just trotted steadily along in the rear, he began to take courage.

'After all,' he said, 'we are three and they are only two. Let us put a good face on the matter, and before nightfall we may yet manage to give them the slip.'

So they kept on their way, chatting together, and affecting to pay no attention to the rats, who followed at a little distance behind them – pad – pad – twitching their whiskers and looking neither to right nor left.

At noon they sat down to rest in the shade of a lofty burdock, making a meal off some wild strawberries which Jensina discovered by the roadside. Not far from them the two rats also waited, panting, and not ill-pleased at the opportunity to rest once more and mop their foreheads. They, however, having no strawberries, could only sit and suck their paws.

'They will soon get tired of this,' Poor Cecco said.

But the rats showed no sign of giving up the chase. All that afternoon they followed on their track, and when twilight fell, and Jensina glanced over her shoulder, it was only to see four green glowing eyes in the distance, following like points of fire through the dusk.

The three friends called a halt to decide what should be done.

'We can't spend the night on the road,' said Jensina. 'At least,' she added, 'not without a campfire.' For her gypsy instincts were still quite strong.

The chance of making a campfire, with no matches, seemed very slight, but in this they were luckier than they expected, for Poor Cecco, who had been sniffing the air eagerly, suddenly exclaimed: 'I smell burning!'

Sure enough, on following him a short distance up the road they found, on a bare space of ground set about with juniper bushes, the remains of a fire which some passing tramp had lighted not long ago. The ashes were still warm, and by blowing on these Jensina, who understood such matters, soon had a nice little blaze started, while Poor Cecco and Bulka gathered twigs and straws for fresh fuel.

It was cheerful to gather round the fire and see the red sparks flying up into the air, and the smoke curling away overhead. The only trouble was, they had nothing to cook by it, and now that darkness had fallen no one felt brave enough to venture out of the circle of firelight to look for food. In fact, though they talked loudly to keep up their courage, they were all three very nervous, and at each sound of a crackling twig, or the rustle of grass in the distance, they looked at one another and drew closer to the blaze.

...like points of fire through the dusk.

But presently their fire began to die down. Suddenly it gave a last little flicker, and went out. Now indeed they were in bad plight!

'This is getting beyond a joke!' said Poor Cecco. 'I must study the situation!'

And he went and lay down by himself at a little distance, with his nose on his paws, thinking.

Jensina and Bulka sat in the long grasses and shivered. Bulka thought of Tubby and the toy-cupboard, and he began to feel very homesick. Big tears rolled down his nose, but he licked them up bravely as fast as they fell, so that Jensina should not see he was crying. The tears came so fast that he had to lick hard to keep up with them, and after a while this occupation in itself proved so exciting that he very nearly forgot his troubles, and when Poor Cecco returned he had just succeeded in catching the last tear of all on the tip of his red flannel tongue, while Jensina sat with her legs stretched straight out before her and her precious bundle on her lap.

CHAPTER 9

You are not invited

'WE must make dummies of grass,' Poor Cecco said, 'and set them up, so that the rats will think they are us, and then we can escape before they find out that they have been tricked!'

'They aren't so stupid as all *that!*' returned Jensina, who was both tired and cross.

'Very well,' said Poor Cecco, 'if you can think of something better perhaps you'll say so. *I'm* not anxious to stay here all night!'

At that very instant an automobile, coming along the road, slowed down just by the spot where the three friends were seated. The driver got out and went forward to attend to his engine, and in the moment that his back was turned Poor Cecco made a hasty sign to Bulka and Jensina. Hopping forward, they were just in time to scramble on to the running-board before the driver returned to his seat and the car started on.

'Where are we going?' said Bulka.

'It doesn't matter where we go,' Poor Cecco replied, 'so long as we get away from the rats, and they certainly can't follow us now.'

'All right!' said Bulka. And being very drowsy, and tired out with the excitement of the day, he at once shut his eyes and went to sleep.

When he awoke the car had stopped again, and Poor Cecco and Jensina, one on each side, were shaking him violently to make him open his eyes.

'Oh, I thought it was morning!' said Bulka, as soon as he could speak. 'Where are we? What are we going to do now?'

'Sh-sh!' said Poor Cecco. 'Keep very quiet and follow us!'

Carrying the bundle, and giving a paw to Jensina, who was stiff and cramped from sitting so long on the running-board, he led them across the road and under a gate into an open field.

'I don't see,' said Jensina, staring about her, 'why you brought us *here!*'

Poor Cecco had no answer to make, for he did not know himself. The field was immense and mountainous and very lonely, lit by a slender moon rising above the hilltop. There were great mounds here and there, and twisted bushes that stood out black in the moonlight, like crouching beasts. Everything looked strange and rather terrible, so that even Poor Cecco's courage began to fail him a little, and he wondered whether after all it wouldn't be better to go back to the road. But here they were, and they must make the best of it, come what might. And while they were still looking about them, wondering which way to go, there was a great whirring of wings, and something dark and huge swept down on them from the sky, striking at Bulka and rolling him over and over on the ground.

Terror seized them; Jensina gave a shriek, but before Poor Cecco could spring to the rescue Bulka had picked himself up again, and there on the grass before them stood an enormous owl, rolling his eyes and looking exactly like a sulky cat.

'How dare you!' cried Poor Cecco.

'How dare *I?*' exclaimed the owl. 'How about him? What business has anyone to go about looking like a rabbit? I couldn't tell! And besides, I didn't hurt him.'

'You did!' squealed Bulka, finding his voice again after the fright. 'You p-pinched me!'

'Cry-baby!' said the owl, contemptuously. He rolled his green eyes at them. 'What are you doing in this field? You aren't real rabbits, any of you! Let me tell you at once, that if you think you can come here under false pretences, and put other people out of business, you're mistaken! I'm the Field-Marshal. I won't stand any nonsense!'

'We are travellers,' said Jensina shrilly, thrusting herself forward.

'We came by automobile, and we have just as much right to be here as you. We are looking for a place to spend the night.'

'Spend it or keep it,' returned the owl. 'It's all one to me. You can suit yourselves. But as for that person' – pointing with his claw at Bulka – 'he'd better wear a label if he doesn't want to get into trouble again.'

'Insufferable creature!' declared Jensina, as the owl flapped heavily away across the field. 'I can't stand owls; they are all the same. Look!' she exclaimed, pointing across the pasture. 'Something is going on over there!'

Something certainly was going on. One of the many hummocks in the field was hung about with twinkling lights, green and pale and golden, and as they drew near they could see that these were countless glowworm lanterns, hung artfully from the grass blades. The effect was both elegant and festive; the whole hummock was a blaze of coloured light, and beside the doorway stood a placard with the words:

'A ball! We must go to this!' cried Jensina, who had lived so long in retirement that the mere prospect of a party made her forget all her weariness. 'I adore dancing, but if it is a formal affair I suppose I had better put on my frock!'

And snatching the bundle from Poor Cecco she hastily unrolled it to get out her dress. She was so anxious to get to the party that she could not even wait to have the frock fastened, but began hopping towards the doorway with one arm thrust through the wrong sleeve hole. 'Let us in!' she cried, and pounded on the door with her fist. 'Let us in! We want to dance!'

The door swung open, and a mole, dressed in black velvet, stood on the threshold. He was plainly one of the ushers, for he wore a white flower in his buttonhole and pink kid gloves.

'What do you want?' he asked.

'We want to dance,' said Jensina, still struggling with her frock, which being hindside before, refused to go over her head.

'Have you an invitation?' asked the mole.

'Certainly we are invited,' returned Poor Cecco, and he pointed to the placard.

'Ah!' said the mole. Stepping outside, he turned the placard round so as to show the other side. It now read, in large clear letters:

And without so much as a further glance at them he went back into the molehill and slammed the door.

'Mean hateful thing!' exclaimed Jensina, ready to cry with disappointment. 'Who wants to go to their old ball anyhow!' And pulling off her frock again she flung it away and sat down hard on the grass, looking very proud and sniffly.

'Never mind,' said Poor Cecco. 'I don't suppose it's much of a dance after all! When we get home, Jensina, we'll have a great ball and only invite whom we want, and there'll be lemonade and a cake with icing, and you shall dance all night long!'

But Jensina was not to be comforted so easily; her pride had been hurt, and moreover she could still hear faintly, through the closed door of the molehill, the scraping of fiddles and the shuffling of feet. So she continued to sit there, sulking on the grass, and to judge by her expression it was far wiser to leave her alone.

As for Bulka, he was dropping with sleep, so Poor Cecco propped him up against Jensina, with the bundle beside them, and set off alone to search for a night's lodging.

CHAPTER 10

The Woodchucks

WANDERING up the hillside, looking here and there, Poor Cecco presently came upon what seemed a very nice cave, warm and dry, and just big enough for the three of them, hollowed out at the foot of a tall rock. Here was luck certainly!

Poor Cecco had always had a passion for caves, and this was quite the best cave he had ever seen, and exactly the right size, whereas caves as a rule are apt to be either too big for cosiness, or else too small to get into, either of which is a serious fault. The sight of this one, he thought, would surely cheer even Jensina up, but as long as Bulka was already asleep, and Jensina probably wouldn't come out of her sulks for another half hour at least, he might as well spend that time in making it still more comfortable. So he went out and began to hunt around in the moonlight for bits of moss and dry grass, enough to make a comfortable bed for all three.

It took quite a little while before he had collected all he needed and sorted it out into heaps, the softest for Jensina, the next best for Bulka, and the hard bits and odds and ends for himself, as he could sleep on anything. When he had got it all together and carried it into the cave, it made such a pile that the cave itself seemed to look smaller, and Poor Cecco decided he might as well make a good job while he was about it, and hollow out the end a little more so as to have plenty of room to sleep in.

While he was scooping busily away with his paws, singing to himself and thinking how nice it would all be when it was finished, all at once he felt a torrent of loose earth raining down on his head; the wall of the cave on which he was working gave way at the same instant, and he fell headlong through.

When he picked himself up, covered with dust and dirt, Poor Cecco found to his surprise that he was in a large and comfortable kitchen. A fat elderly woodchuck, with bushy white whiskers, sat smoking in a corner; his wife, with an apron tied round her enormous waist, was preparing supper at the table, and from a bed in the corner three small woodchucks, equally fat, poked their heads out, each with a white nightcap on, to see what had happened. All five stared at Poor Cecco in astonishment and some indignation, for it is certainly not usual for a total stranger to drop in on one suddenly through the kitchen ceiling at supper-time, especially when he brings half the ceiling with him, as Poor Cecco had unfortunately done.

The old woodchuck took his pipe from his mouth and stared from the hole in the ceiling to Poor Cecco, and back at the ceiling again, unable to say a word, while his whiskers bristled more and more, his eyes grew rounder and rounder, and his whole body swelled up as if he were going to burst.

At last he recovered sufficiently to say, in a very angry voice:

'Wipe your feet when you come in at the door!'

This seemed to Poor Cecco unnecessary, considering he had come by the roof, but as he felt himself to be in the wrong, in any case, he began at once to excuse himself for his entrance.

'Rubbish!' said the woodchuck. 'No sensible person keeps their front door in the ceiling! When you don't see what you want, ask for it, and don't go blundering about like that!'

Mrs Woodchuck, who had said nothing all this while, but after one glance went on calmly slicing vegetables, now addressed her husband without looking up.

'It's all your own shiftlessness!' she said. 'Didn't I tell you a dozen times, if I've told you once, that if you wouldn't hike yourself up there and do something to that roof before the bad weather set in anything was liable to beat in on us? But there you set, and if the house itself fell in you wouldn't lift a finger except to blame someone else. Don't talk to me about it!'

Mr Woodchuck, at this, seemed to sink down in his chair. He cast a timid glance at his wife, and hastily putting the pipe back in his mouth began to smoke again in great puffs. Mrs Woodchuck, who had now finished slicing her last carrot, swept all the vegetables into a yellow bowl which she set down on the table with a slam, before turning to Poor Cecco.

'Sit down, young man,' she said, 'if you can find a place, and let me tell you at once we never subscribe to anything. I have no aches nor pains in my back, and we all bought new toothbrushes last week.'

'I didn't come to sell anything,' said Poor Cecco, rather bewildered. 'I dropped in quite by accident!' And he began to explain to Mrs Woodchuck, who seemed the more sensible of the two, how he came to be in the cave, and about Jensina and Bulka, whom he had left behind in the field.

'Then in that case,' said Mrs Woodchuck briskly, 'the best thing you can do is to fetch your two friends and spend the night here, if the young lady isn't too particular. We are simple folk and you must take us as you find us. We get along somehow. Luckily the farmer is keeping a better garden this year, and my old man gets a job when he can, but the lumber trade has been slack lately. The last few months I've had to take in washing to help out; to tell the truth the whole house if full up with it now and that's why we've so little room. We've even had to move the beds into the kitchen, as you can see for yourself; I was thinking only today, I don't see how I can possibly take in any more, do what I will, there's no space left for it anywhere!'

Looking about him, Poor Cecco saw that every corner of the room was piled with bundles of laundry, each tied up just as it had come from the owner; in fact there was very little space left anywhere, and he thought at once that Mrs Woodchuck would do better, instead of taking so much washing in, to send some of it out again, and he told her so.

'I know!' said Mrs Woodchuck, untying her apron and rolling it into a ball which she flung under the table. 'I know – I've thought so myself at times, but what can I do? There's so much to look after in this house that I never get a minute, and besides – I hate washing. I was never brought up to it! And now,' she continued, 'you had better go and fetch your friends and we'll have a little supper.'

Mr Woodchuck led Poor Cecco to the real doorway, down a passage so stacked with washing on either side that the woodchuck, being extremely fat, had great difficulty in squeezing past. 'You see how it is,' he whispered hoarsely, pointing with his pipe. 'We're being pushed out of house and home, and to hear the old woman talk you'd think no one did a hand's turn but herself!'

Poor Cecco ran down the hill, glad to be in the open air again. The ball was over; the lights were turned out, the placard taken in, and the door of the molehill shut fast. Jensina and Bulka were both sound asleep, leaning on each other's shoulders; he had some difficulty in rousing them. Bulka in fact scarcely woke at all. He stumbled drowsily up the hill, dragging the string of beads to which he had clung through all his adventures, and when they reached the house Poor Cecco pushed him in at once, head first, among the baby woodchucks, who had pulled the quilt over their heads and were snoring soundly.

Jensina, however, aroused when she found herself in the kitchen, and became quite lively. She gossiped with Mrs Woodchuck, set the table, washed the dishes and brushed off the crumbs, and altogether made herself most agreeable. And then, weariness overcoming her suddenly, she stretched out on the floor and was immediately fast asleep.

Poor Cecco, who was in no mind to give up the beautiful cave he had taken so much trouble over, went up and spent the night there alone.

He was awakened by the smell of coffee, and the voices of Jensina and Mrs Woodchuck, who were conversing in the kitchen below him, Mrs Woodchuck saying: 'For my part I like my coffee strong, and as for my husband, he will touch nothing but the very best acorns!'

'That sounds like breakfast!' thought Poor Cecco, and he rose, stretched himself, and trotted round to the front door.

Jensina, who was a born housewife, had been at work early. The kitchen was swept, the beds made, and coffee steaming on the table. Mrs Woodchuck had dressed the children, and being shortsighted, insisted on buttoning Bulka into the velvet jacket belonging to Ferdinand, the youngest woodchuck, who thereupon burst into loud howls, but the mistake was soon remedied.

After breakfast they were prepared to start on their way, but Mrs Woodchuck, who was a most hospitable soul, would not hear of this. She had arranged, she said, to invite a few neighbours in that evening to make a little party for Jensina, and it would be too bad to disappoint them.

In return for her kindness Jensina immediately offered to lend a hand with the washing while Mrs Woodchuck made her preparations for the party. So she set off for the spring, a bundle under each arm, leaving Poor Cecco and Bulka to bring as many more as they could carry, for, she said, one might as well make a good job of it.

The spring was a little distance below the house, in a hollow set about with tall shady grasses. All that Bulka and Poor Cecco need do, therefore, was to stand at the top of the hill and roll the bundles down to her as fast as she needed them, which they did while Jensina spent her day kneeling at the edge of the spring, splashing merrily about and very contented. By tea-time she had washed one hundred and thirteen bundles of laundry, which was certainly, she thought, some little help to her hostess, and as all the water in the spring was now used up it was as well to stop.

So having hung her laundry neatly out to dry on the grasses, she smoothed her hair, dried her hands on a mullein leaf, and went back to the house to await the party.

CHAPTER II

Jensina's party

THE first to arrive were Mr and Mrs Weasel, and their friends the Chipmunks. Old Ezra Bunny came next with his family, and then the High-Hangers, who wore red waistcoats and were rather superior, Mrs Fieldmouse, and the Opossums, who were new to the neighbourhood. They had just taken a house in the woodlot across the hill and were anxious to be thought well of, though many considered them humbugs. Then came Auntie Skunk and Uncle Billie Skunk and their four children, and by this time the kitchen was quite full. Thanks to Jensina's industry most of the laundry bundles had disappeared, except a few which, arranged to look like sofas and chairs, did very well for the company to sit upon. Mrs Woodchuck's guests tried to appear politely unaware of the real nature of the furniture beneath them; only Mrs Weasel, seeing a fragment of brown calico peeping out, was heard to remark impulsively:

'There's my petticoat I've missed for three months! I do wish she'd send the things back if she's ever going to!'

Acorn coffee was served, with nuts and carrot sandwiches, and then the babies of the party were all put to bed, not without some trouble, in an adjoining closet, and while the old folks settled themselves in a corner the dancing began.

Uncle Billie Skunk played the fiddle, and old Ezra Bunny the concertina. Old Ezra wore a white shirtfront and a brown coat, rather untidy in the seams, and he had long yellow teeth that showed whenever he smiled. He had played for so many kitchen dances that he could call out the figures with his eyes shut. He waved the concertina over his head and stamped with his foot whenever it was time for the music to change.

'First couples forward!' he called out. 'Ladies in the middle! Swing your partners!' And while he stamped and shouted Uncle Billie Skunk, all in black, looked very solemn as he bent over his fiddle, but was really winking at the dancers all the time.

'It's a lovely party!' Jensina whispered to Poor Cecco as they whirled round the floor. 'I'm so glad we stayed!'

Jensina, in her gingham frock, and wearing the blue beads which Bulka had lent her for the evening, was very much admired and enjoyed herself thoroughly. It quite made up, in fact, for her disappointment of the night before. Among these simple people she found herself quite at ease, and behaved accordingly. She danced gypsy dances, sang songs and told fortunes, and in the intervals of the music had always a little group about her. Indeed, it was whispered before the evening was over that the eldest High-Hanger would have proposed marriage to her, had he not been already engaged to a distant cousin on the Woodpecker branch of the family.

Bulka was also having a delightful time. He had made friends with the young Chipmunks, and they were enjoying a dance of their own at the farther end of the kitchen. Not knowing the steps, they held hands in a ring while each capered as he chose in time to the music. Presently, Bulka, losing his shyness, grew excited. He pushed his companions aside, and having cleared a space all to himself on the floor, began to turn somersaults and stand on his head.

Poor Cecco attended to everyone, showed new steps to his partners, and in the intervals carried sandwiches to the old ladies in the corner, entreating them to get up and dance with him.

'His manners are perfect,' murmured Mrs Chipmunk, 'and he is so distinguished. He arrived with his party last night by automobile. They are making a tour of the world. The young lady they say is of gypsy extraction and most talented; she told my fortune in the coffee-cup and it was quite surprising! I am to become famous and inherit a large fortune!'

'Perhaps then she won't need to steal other people's nuts in the Fall,' whispered the fieldmouse to her neighbour.

Presently there was a knock at the door, and Mr Woodchuck hastened to open. It was the Iron Grenadier from the farm across the way. He had begun life as a door-weight, but losing his position and the greater part of his substance with it, by an accident in middle age, had since spent his declining years in the barn. He was old and very stiff, but on hearing that a party was to be given in honour of the strangers he came stumping up the hill, pounding on every door in turn and shouting enquiries, until at last he found Mrs Woodchuck's house.

He was given at once the place of honour by the chimneyside, with a mug of blackberry cider and Mr Woodchuck's best pipe.

'A bit of a bore,' Mrs Weasel whispered to Poor Cecco, 'and he shouts so loudly it's quite dreadful at times, but he is a solid character, and we all feel proud of him!'

Suddenly, while the enjoyment was at its height, and Jensina had just performed for the third time her most dashing gypsy dance,

twirling on her toes and snapping her fingers, there was a strange and sinister scuffling overhead, accompanied by loud squeaks. And immediately, through the hole in the roof which Mr Woodchuck had still forgotten to repair, something fell with a thud right at Jensina's very feet.

It was a large stone, with a piece of paper wrapped around it. Poor Cecco was the first to snatch it up, and when he had unfolded the paper this is what they saw:

Instantly the music stopped. Everyone crowded round. 'What is it?' they cried. 'What is it?' Mrs Chipmunk put her hand to her heart, and Bulka left off turning somersaults and pushed forward to see what had happened.

As for Jensina, when the stone fell at her feet, she stood for a moment perfectly still, as though turned to a statue. Now, at sight of the writing on the paper, she became deathly pale.

'She is fainting!' someone cried. 'Bring her water!'

But Jensina controlled herself, and with a despairing look flung her arms round the necks of Poor Cecco and Bulka, who happened to be nearest to her.

'Alas, my friends!' she sobbed. 'Alas! It is I who have brought all this trouble upon you!'

'Stop crying!' ordered Poor Cecco, who disliked being hugged in public. 'Tell me at once, Jensina, what this means? For I think,' he added sternly, 'you know more about this business than you told us, and I suspected all along you had something up your sleeve!'

'It isn't up my sleeve,' said Jensina. 'It is – but stay! Who knows what ears may be listening? How much better if I had never deceived you, but told you the whole truth from the beginning!'

'It certainly would!' said Poor Cecco, while Bulka, who hated to see anyone cry except himself, uttered hastily: 'Don't be cross to her!'

Jensina, however, had stopped weeping. Sitting down on the floor, and drying her eyes with the edge of her frock, she began:

'When I first came to live among the ash-heaps where you met me I was very lonely. For long weeks I saw no one to speak to. I've always been used to company, and little by little, if only to pass the time of day, I was forced to make acquaintance with the rats. They were the only people living there, I was quite at their mercy, and I had to be polite. There was one among them, lame in the hind leg and better mannered than the others, who had been kind to me in the beginning, and he used to come sometimes of an evening and drink a cup of coffee at my house. It was from him I learned the few words of rat language that I know.

'Being too lame for active service, my friend – for I may call him that – was employed in the government, and he told me from time to time a great deal about the customs and traditions of the rat people. Much that he told me was both curious and strange – in fact I think he talked a lot more than he should have done – and having a high position in the Secret Service he knew many things that are hidden from the ordinary rat in the street. Among other things, he told me of the existence of the rats' most treasured possession, the Tooth of Grimalkin.'

On hearing Jensina refer to the ash-heap country, in that matter-of-fact way, some of the company who had been foremost in admiring her during the evening, now turned up their noses; and began at once to look about for their wraps; but at word 'treasure' their curiosity got the better of them, and they sat down again, though not without some whispering among themselves, to which, however, Jensina paid no heed.

'This object,' Jensina continued, 'has been in the rats' keeping for many centuries and is most jealously guarded. In times of peace its place is in the King's treasury, and in war-time it is carried before them in public procession. It is said to have come into their possession in the time of the Mousades, when their hero slew the cat Grimalkin and bore back the Tooth in trophy. As long as they preserve this mascot, so the rats believe, no enemy can overcome them, but without it they would at once become powerless. No rat can gaze on this precious relic unmoved; few in fact ever have the chance to do so anyway, but my friend was among these few, and so he was able to describe the Tooth to me in complete detail.

'Now I must tell you,' Jensina went on, considerably cheered by having an audience, 'that in spite of their cleverness the rats are really very careless. Their archives, as my friend admitted, are often kept in a terrible state; everything in disorder and they don't even trouble about repairs. As one of their proverbs says, "Good is good enough." So it happened on thc night of the great storm, which you will remember, when the sky broke and all the water came tumbling down, the cellars of the Royal Treasure were completely flooded, and it fell to the lot of one rat, the janitor's brother-in-law, who happened to be on guard, to rush down, snatch the box containing the relic, and bear it to a place of safety.

'Now, whether there was a hole in the box, which I can quite believe, knowing their extreme carelessness in such matters, or whether the guardian in his hurry carried it upside down, I don't know. But on going for a walk first thing in the morning, to see what was washed out by the storm, the first thing I saw, shining on the path before me, was the famous Tooth of Grimalkin.

'On the moment's impulse I picked it up and hid it under my frock, meaning to give it back to my friend at the first opportunity. But when you arrived I was so overjoyed at meeting persons of my own rank once more that the Tooth went completely out of my head.

'Later, I slipped it in my bundle, still meaning to leave it in some spot where it might be found. But the behaviour of the rats, and their horrid attack on dear Bulka, at once altered my mind. Disgusted with them, I decided that they could hunt their tooth for themselves, but at a certain moment, seeing that the battle was going against us, and wishing to divert their attention, I was rash enough to call out in rat language: 'Go and look after your precious old Grimalkin Tooth!'

'You saw' – she turned to Bulka and Poor Cecco – 'the immediate effect of my words! I admit it surprised me, for up to then I hadn't really believed all I was told. But it was too late; the secret was out, and I was determined that, come what might, never would I give up that tooth, if only to spite them, and I hurried you away in the hope that we might yet outdistance their pursuit. But alas, no such luck!'

'Ash-heaps, indeed, and picking up what doesn't belong to her!' sniffed Mrs Weasel aloud. 'I always said the Woodchucks kept queer company! It's time we went home, before there's trouble with the police!'

Fortunately Jensina didn't hear her remark, but Mrs Woodchuck did, and was rightly indignant.

'You may go home, you stuck-up things!' she cried heartily. 'And small credit to you! Your washing will be returned tomorrow, and I'll thank you to pay at the door!'

Saying which she bustled them out, and the High-Hangers with them, before turning to Jensina and exclaiming: 'Poor darling, with all the trouble she's been through!'

'It isn't *that* I mind,' said Jensina, dabbing at her eyes again. 'I'd go through it again tomorrow just to spite those rats, but it's the trouble I have brought on my friends by my own pig-headedness. And now I'm in a terrible hole, for if I give the Tooth back to them for the sake of peace they'll only take their revenge on us, and as long as I keep it, so long will they pursue us and track us down, as they did tonight. Oh, dear! Oh, dear!' And she nearly broke down again.

The Iron Grenadier seemed to have been asleep all this while, but in reality he had been listening attentively to all that Jensina said. Clearing his voice now, he began:

'My dear young lady, this is a matter in which an old soldier's advice may be very useful. In the first place, I have heard many times of this famous Tooth of Grimalkin, for the legend of it exists wherever the rat people dwell. Living in the barn I am in touch with what goes on, and I may tell you that up to now the Rat Government have kept their loss very secret, for no rumour of it has reached the rats in this part of the country. This is good news for you, as it shows that they dread exposure and realise their helplessness, but for which they would have attacked you long ago. As long as you keep the Tooth you are safe; they may try to trick you and frighten you into giving it up, but they will not dare to attack you openly. You have therefore a dangerous and most powerful weapon, and one you must use with care. To give it up, at this point, would be fatal, and very silly. You must keep it till such time as you may happen to need the rats' help; then you can drive a bargain with them. Use prudence and all your wit, and have no fear that in such conditions as you impose, they will keep their word.

'And now it is time that we all took a little rest, and if you feel any nervousness, remember I am an old campaigner, and I shall have the greatest pleasure in standing guard at your doorway all night!'

And after gallantly kissing Jensina's hand, the party having by now dispersed, he took up his station outside the front door and stayed there sternly, musket in hand, till the sun rose and the dew stood out in shining drops on his iron nose.

CHAPTER 12

The lettuce box

'THE best thing to do,' said Poor Cecco next morning, when they had bidden the Woodchucks good-bye and were walking down the hill, 'is to go home. This life of adventure is all very well, but we have been away for a long time, and by now everyone will be wondering what has become of us.'

'Home!' shouted Bulka. 'Hurray! Let's go home!' And he turned a somersault at once.

It was all very well to say, but how would they get there? It wasn't so easy. For one thing, no one had the faintest idea, now, in which direction home lay. It might be East, West, North or South, but after taking so many turns and coming through so many adventures even

Poor Cecco had lost his sense of direction completely. As for Bulka, he had never even troubled his head about anything of the kind.

Poor Cecco thought and thought, and in the end he took a piece of stick, and finding a smooth bit of earth began to trace on it, as well as he could remember, the way they had come. It looked a queer sort of map when he had done, with stones and scraps of twig stuck in here and there to mark the different points of their journey, and certainly no one but Poor Cecco himself could have explained it.

'First,' he said, 'we came down a road, and here is the bridge, and the old man, and those pebbles are the ducks – there ought to be more of them, but never mind – and that twisty line is the river. And then we crossed a field, only I can't make that very well because it was all dark, but somewhere *there* is the little dog's cottage, and this is the ash-heap country, and that white stone is Jensina. And here is where the rats attacked us, and then we went back to the road again. Stop a minute – I must put the road farther over; there isn't room. And then we took the automobile.'

Ah, the automobile! That was the real trouble. No one knew which way the automobile had gone. For one thing, they were half asleep most of the way. Certainly the automobile mixed everything up. If it hadn't been for that, Poor Cecco was quite sure his map would have come out all right.

'Let's leave the automobile out,' suggested Bulka.

'We can't,' said Poor Cecco. 'The automobile must have gone this way.' And he traced another line.

'But it would have gone straight into the long grass!' Bulka objected.

'Don't be silly!' said Poor Cecco. 'Can't you see it's only a map? The question is, where are we now?'

'That isn't the question at all,' put in Jensina, rather snappily, for she was getting bored with watching Poor Cecco stick in his twigs and stones. 'I know perfectly well where we are *now*. I'm not an idiot! What I want to know is where we are *going*.'

'Can't you have patience?' Poor Cecco exclaimed. 'All you can put in a map are the places you've already been. That's what a map's for. No one ever heard of a map that showed the places people haven't been yet. There'd be no sense to it.'

'There's no sense to this,' said Jensina, 'so far as I can see! Look where you've put the river – just where Bulka's going to step in it!'

Bulka drew back, alarmed, but seeing only a line on the earth, stepped over it, and wandered off to look for huckleberries. Someone would have to find the way home; it didn't trouble him.

Poor Cecco folded his legs and lay down sulkily. He thought it was too bad of Jensina to be so critical when he really was trying his best.

Suddenly Jensina sat up and thumped the ground.

'Listen! I have an idea!'

'Well?' said Poor Cecco, still sulky.

'Do you know the name of your house?'

'What do you mean?' asked Poor Cecco. 'It's just called the house.'

'Do you know what house it is?' Jensina explained.

'Of course I do!' said Poor Cecco.

'Then if you can write what house it is,' Jensina cried. 'And if we've got three pennies, we'll go back by R.F.D.'

Poor Cecco pricked up his ears.

'What's that?'

'It's a man in a car,' said Jensina, 'and he rides up and down the world all day taking things where they have to go. He's *got* to take them. And whatever you write the name of the place on he's got to take it there.'

'But why is he called R.F.D.?' Poor Cecco asked.

Jensina thought a moment. 'R.F.D. means Rides For Dolls, of course,' she returned, very superior. 'Everyone knows that.'

'It might mean Rides for Dogs,' said Poor Cecco, who didn't see why Jensina should have it all her own way.

Just then Bulka poked his head up through the long grass. 'Who's going to ride?' he asked.

'All of us!' said Jensina promptly. 'Dear me, Bulka, you do look a sight! Brush all that grass-seed off you, do, and Poor Cecco find a clean piece of paper, and we'll write the address.'

Bulka had been hunting huckleberries in the pasture. He hadn't found one, but he had found a great many other things instead – hayseed and dried leaves and bits of twig and burrs – which were sticking all over him, and while he sat down obediently and began to pick them off, one by one, Poor Cecco found a clean bit of pasteboard, from a cigarette packet someone had thrown away, and dipping a twig into blackberry juice he began to write, while Jensina looked over his shoulder.

This is what he wrote, in a fine round hand:

THE-WOODEN-HOUSE-
WITH-TWO-TREES-
IN-FRONT

Left-hand corner of the road

Going to Strawberryville

It looked very well when he had done, but Poor Cecco was still a little doubtful.

'Do you think he'll find it?' he asked.

'Of course he'll find it,' said Jensina. 'That's what he's for. And now we must go and wait by the letters-box.'

So, Bulka being by now fairly tidy, Poor Cecco tucked the label under his arm, and with Jensina carrying her precious bundle they all three made their way under the pasture bars and back to the road. And sure enough, before they had gone very far, there was a grey box on a post by the roadside with R.F.D. written on it, just as Jensina had said.

'You see I was right!' she exclaimed. 'Here is the letters-box, and if you'll help me up all we've got to do is to sit here till the letter-man comes by.'

Poor Cecco climbed up first, by the help of a vine that twined about the post, and with a little pushing and pulling they were soon all three seated up there, safe and sound, with their legs dangling over the edge.

Jensina set up the flag, to be sure the letter-man would stop for them, while Bulka, leaning over, peered into the box.

'I don't see any lettuce!' he cried.

'Where?' Jensina asked.

'In the box. You *said* it was a lettuce box!'

'It's not *that* kind of lettuce,' explained Jensina. 'I said letters-box, where they post the letters!'

'There's only one kind,' returned Bulka, offended. 'I see the post all right, but there's no lettuce. I'm hungry! I'm going back to look for huckleberries again.'

'You can't!' cried Jensina, and she caught him by one leg just as he was getting ready to slide down. 'You mustn't be hungry, Bulka. We're going home!'

At the word 'home' Bulka ceased to resist, and sat down again beside them. For safety Jensina made him sit in the middle with the address label across his tummy, and then, taking a piece of pink string she had picked up by the roadside, she bound them all three firmly

together, in case, as she explained, they might get separated on the journey.

The three pennies, taken from the bundle, were laid on the letter-box beside them. It was agreed that Bulka should pay his own fare, while Poor Cecco would pay for himself and Jensina. Thus there was exactly one penny, belonging to Poor Cecco, left over.

It was not very pleasant waiting there, for the sun beat down on their heads and the iron top of the letter-box soon became uncomfortably hot to sit upon; in fact it was almost like an oven. Poor Cecco had the idea of picking some leaves from the vine that grew near, and with these they contrived parasols to keep the glare from their faces.

'I wish the letter-man would hurry!' said Jensina, examining her painted shoes, which were beginning to blister from the sun.

Bulka was asleep, as usual.

Presently, however, a little cloud of dust appeared far away on the road. It was the letter-man's car, and at length, with much banging and rattling, it drew up before them. The driver was a pleasant-faced man. He stared hard at the little party sitting, all tied together, on the top of the letter-box, and he scratched his head.

'That's a queer sort of a parcel!' he said.

Still, the label was there, in Poor Cecco's beautiful round handwriting, and the pennies were there, so he had no choice but to pick them up, which he did rather gingerly and set them on the seat beside him, after first licking three stamps and sticking them, one on Poor Cecco's forehead, one on Bulka's forehead, and one on Jensina's.

Then the car went on its way, rattling and bumping, to the next letter-box.

Scarcely had it started before two rats poked their noses from the tall weeds behind the post, and with one swift glance about them, set out on a steady businesslike trot along the road.

CHAPTER 13

Murrum's revenge

WHAT had been happening at home all this while?

When the others woke up in the morning they rushed at once to the dolls' cradle, and seeing the stick of wood lying there wrapped up in the blankets, they had a great shock. It really looked as if something dreadful had happened to Poor Cecco! Perhaps he had died in the night! But when they unrolled the covers and saw it was only a stick of firewood after all, and just another of Poor Cecco's tricks, they were pretty angry. He had no business to go away and leave them like that, and worse still, he had taken Bulka with him.

Poor Cecco often disappeared; they were used to that. Very likely he had just gone off early to get himself a new tail, to surprise them with. But Bulka was another matter; Bulka had never been known to go away before.

Tubby in particular was very upset. She remembered how she had quarrelled with Bulka the night before, and called him a cry-baby. Now he had gone, and all her tears would not bring him back.

All that day she sat in a corner, and thought of the terrible things that might be happening to him, one worse than another. Even Ida, with all her soothing ways, could not console her. If Bulka ever came back, Tubby thought, she would tell him how much she really loved him. But she couldn't wait for that; she must write a letter, before she forgot all the things that she wanted to say, and after hunting about for a scrap of paper and a stub of lead pencil she seated herself in a corner behind the coal-scuttle and began to write.

> DEAR BULKA:
> I love you and I sorry I called you a cry-baby and if you come back I will make you ice-cream and a cake with ammons on and I'll take you to Tubbyland
> Yours loving
> TUBBY.

That looked very nice, but not quite nice enough, so sticking her tongue out carefully she began again.

> DEAR BULKA:
> I miss you very much and if you come back I will make you a orange cake with icing and ammons on top and I love you and I hope you come back. there is no more nues at present with love from
> TUBBY.

The third was like this:

> DEAR BULKA:
> I love you more than the sky and more than the blue and when you come back I will make you a cake with

orange icing and ammons and silver balls and you are not a cry-baby

TUBBY.

PS I love you more than Christmas and Easter and Fairyland

By the evening Tubby had written thirty-seven letters and had used up nearly all the paper out of the wastepaper basket. She folded the letters very small and sealed them S.W.A.K. Where to post them was the question, but after thinking a little while Tubby decided what to do. She gathered up all the letters in her pinafore, and creeping up very quietly, she posted them all inside the Money-Pig while he wasn't looking.

Now she had no more paper, but the Easter Chicken settled that. He came running up, dragging a nearly clean paper bag which he had found by the pantry door.

'Here's paper, Tubby!' he cried. 'I'll find you all the paper you want! I know where there's a whole lot of it!'

So, greatly cheered, Tubby settled down once more to her letter-writing. So deep was she in her task, clutching the pencil tightly and with a tip of her tongue stuck out, that she never even heard the other toys calling her.

They were going on a picnic.

'Where's Tubby?' asked Anna, when Tubby didn't answer.

'Sh-sh!' returned Gladys. 'She's behind the coal-scuttle, writing letters to Bulka.'

Tubby heard this, but she made no sound, only turned very red and went on with her letter.

'Well, we needn't bother about her,' said Virginia May. 'If she doesn't want to come she can stay behind.'

And they all set off, with a great clatter and shouting, as usual; all except the Easter Chicken and the Money-Pig, who complained of indigestion and wanted to sleep. No wonder, with all those letters inside him!

The house grew very still and lonely, but Tubby didn't mind. She sat and wrote; her pencil went scratch-scratch busily on the paper without stopping. She was writing Bulka all the most lovely things she could think of. It is true that her letters were all rather alike, but that didn't matter; one can't always be saying something different. She was having a wonderful time. And meanwhile the Easter Chicken ran to and fro, fetching Tubby all the scraps of paper he could find, and as soon as each letter was finished he went over on tiptoe and posted it in the Money-Pig.

Ding-dong! chimed the clock, twelve times. A beam of moonlight came through the window. It moved slowly nearer, till it lit up the dark corner behind the coal-scuttle where Tubby sat writing. A tear stood on her nose, for at that moment she was wondering where Bulka was, and the thought that something might have happened to him, and that perhaps he would never read the letters she had written, was almost too much for her. But there was no use dwelling on dreadful thoughts, so she rubbed the tear off with her pencil and went on writing more busily than ever.

A shadow moved in the far corner by the door. It was Murrum, just returned through the kitchen window from his prowling. He caught sight of Tubby sitting there in the moonlight, and pricked up his ears.

Murrum was in a very bad temper. Things were going from bad to worse. He had not caught a single mouse in the last three nights. He blamed this entirely on the toys, and for a long time he had been planning revenge. Only this very day he had gone his rounds, sniffing everywhere; there was just one hole in the room, he knew, where a mouse might possibly be, and as luck would have it that hole was exactly in the corner by the fireplace, behind the coal-scuttle, where Tubby sat writing her letters.

Murrum's tail twitched angrily. It was too bad! There she sat, right in his way. 'Stop rustling that paper!' he growled. 'What are you doing there?'

'I won't tell you,' said Tubby, and her pencil went straight on – scratch – scratch – on the paper.

'You're making a noise!' cried Murrum. 'How dare you? Get out of my corner at once!'

Tubby made no answer, though the Easter Chicken plucked anxiously at her skirt. Murrum's tail was twitching to and fro, and his eyes shone like green lamps.

'Will you get out from there?' he hissed.

'No,' said Tubby. 'I won't. So Hinksman!'

This was more than Murrum could endure. He made one furious bound, and seized Tubby then and there by the neck. The Easter Chicken gave a piteous squawk, but there was no one to hear. In two jumps Murrum crossed the floor and was out through the kitchen window, with Tubby in his mouth. Down the path he sped, and across the parsley border to the big willow tree in the corner by the fence, and climbing up the trunk he dropped poor Tubby – plong – right down the dark hole in the middle!

'*Now* we'll see,' said Murrum, 'who's master in this house!'

CHAPTER 14

Where is Tubby?

THE poor Easter Chicken did not know which way to turn. He rushed to the Money-Pig and shook him violently.

The Money-Pig, who had seen everything that happened, pretended to be asleep. He was really a terrible coward.

'Leave me alone!' he grumbled. 'What's the matter?'

'Tubby!' cried the Easter Chicken. 'Murrum has carried off Tubby!'

'I'll say she deserved it!' said the Money-Pig. 'I can't do anything, can I?'

But the Easter Chicken continued to beat him with his wings, shouting: 'Tubby's gone! You must wake up! Murrum has stolen her!'

'Can't you leave me alone?' the Money-Pig complained. 'Isn't it enough that you must be stuffing goodness knows what all down my back all day! It isn't money, I'm sure; I never felt so sick in my life. If Tubby's gone, good riddance! I'm not going to worry about her. Let me sleep, for goodness' sake. Oh, dear! Oh, dear!' And he pretended to groan.

Just then the rest of the party returned from their picnic. They trooped in laughing, chattering and shouting, making such a noise that it was several minutes before the Easter Chicken could even make himself heard, though he did his best, running from one to another, flapping his wings and chirping piteously.

'What's the matter?' asked Gladys at last. 'What's all this fuss? You should have been in bed hours ago!'

'Tubby's gone! Tubby's gone!' the Easter Chicken cried. And he poured out a story in which Tubby, Murrum and the Money-Pig were so mixed up that Gladys could make out nothing at all.

'Come here!' she called to the others. 'What's he fussing about, do you suppose? He's got some silly idea in his head but I can't understand a word of it!'

'It's Tubby!' he sobbed.

'Well, what about Tubby?' asked Virginia May tartly, for she had been interrupted in a conversation with Harlequin, and Harlequin's conversations were rare.

'Tubby has gone!' said the Easter Chicken.

'Is that all? Well, she's gone to Tubbyland, I suppose! She's done it dozens of times before,' said Gladys. 'Nothing to get so excited about.'

For it had long been Tubby's habit, especially when she felt herself slighted, to retire into hiding in some spot known only to herself, and from which she would reappear later, telling everyone, with a most superior air, that she had just been to Tubbyland – a habit which annoyed the rest of the Toys unutterably, for they none of them really believed her.

'She'll come back when she gets tired of it,' said Anna wisely. 'Stop chattering so much. Little chickens should be seen and not heard!'

'But she hasn't gone to Tubbyland,' the Easter Chicken insisted. 'I tell you she's stolen! Murrum stole her!'

'*Now* you're telling fibs!' exclaimed Virginia May severely. 'You know you are always making things up. I don't believe you.'

'He's had a nightmare,' suggested the Lion. 'Go back to bed, Chicken, and keep quiet!'

'But it's true! It's true! The Money-Pig saw him!'

'I didn't!' cried the Money-Pig hastily, for he was afraid of being blamed. 'I was fast asleep. He woke me up. I'm feeling very unwell!'

'Of *course* she's gone to Tubbyland!' said Gladys. 'She was always talking about it. Besides, no one's seen Murrum for two days.'

But at the word 'Murrum' an uncomfortable chill fell on the party. However boldly they might talk when they were together, there was not one of them would have liked to meet Murrum alone, especially at night, unless it was Poor Cecco, and Poor Cecco was away. They shifted their feet and looked at one another uneasily. If only Poor Cecco were here this question would soon be settled. Meantime, if only to try and pacify the Easter Chicken, they began to hunt about for Tubby.

They looked behind the sofa cushions, and under the sideboard, even inside the coal-scuttle itself, but there was no Tubby to be seen. High and low they searched, calling her, but it was all no use. Now indeed they began to get alarmed.

'She's doing it on purpose,' said Virginia May, trying not to feel frightened. 'It's all because we made fun of her writing letters to Bulka.'

'I wish Poor Cecco were here!' said Harlequin sadly. And Anna began to snivel. 'Things always seem to go wrong when Poor Cecco's away!'

No use wishing for Poor Cecco! They must do their best without him. All the rest of that night, led by Harlequin and the Lion, they hunted and called. They even turned back the carpet and poked out the cracks in the kitchen floor with hairpins. There was no trace of

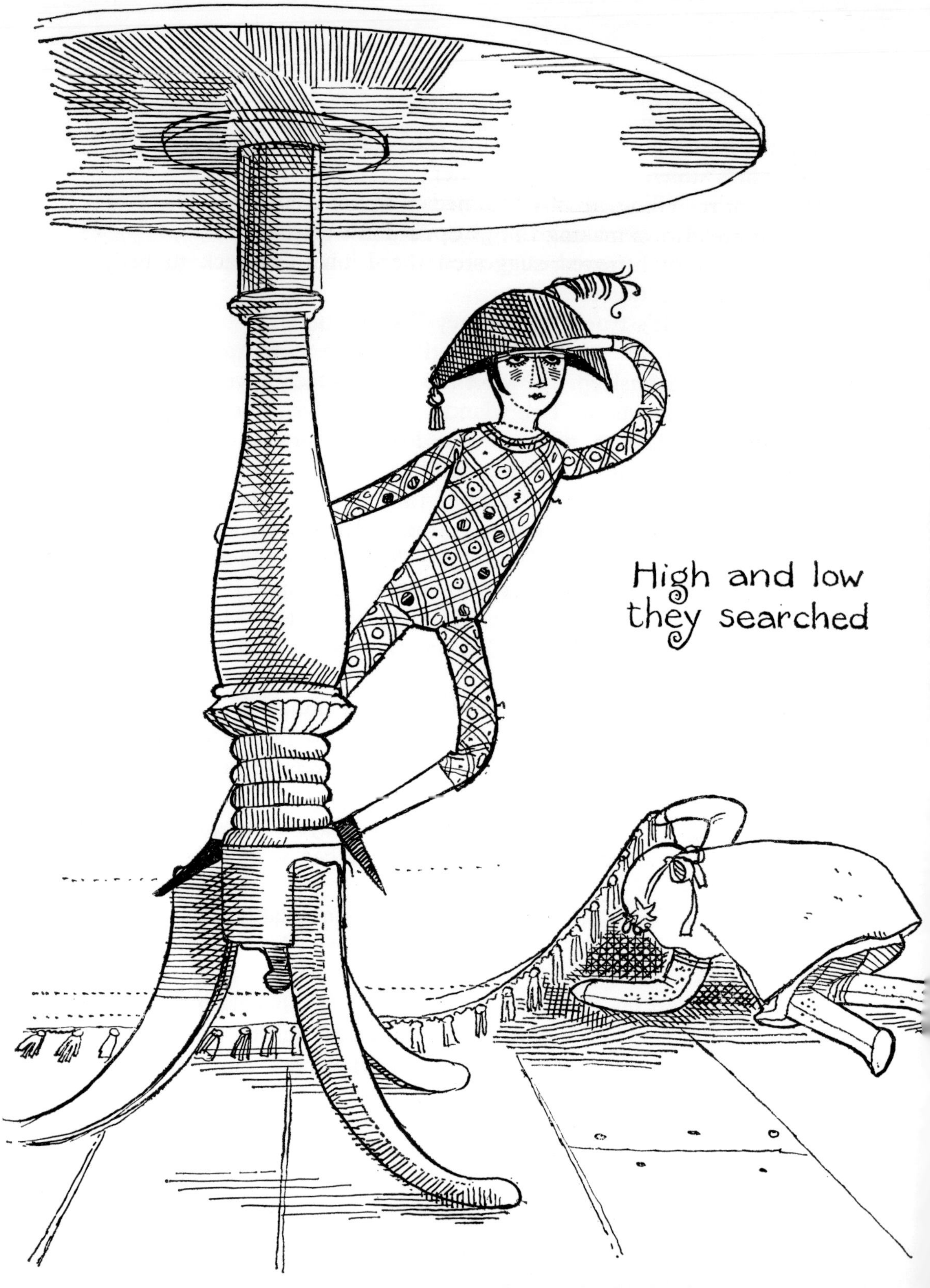

High and low
they searched

Tubby anywhere, except a few torn scraps of paper behind the coal-scuttle.

It was a very dejected party that gathered in the toy-cupboard next morning. Never before had Tubby remained hidden so long. And though Gladys and Anna still maintained she had only gone to Tubbyland, the rest of them began to feel certain by now that something had happened. As for the Easter Chicken, he had sobbed himself to sleep long ago.

The toys woke him up, for they felt that someone had to be blamed for the whole affair.

'Why didn't you stop Murrum?' they scolded. 'You ought to have called us. You should have told someone!'

'I told the Money-Pig!'

'You didn't!' the Money-Pig shouted, and immediately closed his eyes again and groaned.

Certainly something had given him indigestion. But the other toys were too worried to pay any attention to his troubles.

'You'll catch it when Poor Cecco comes back!' said Harlequin darkly. And the Engine and Anna and the dolls all cried: 'Yes, it's all your fault!'

That didn't frighten the Easter Chicken. All he cared about was rescuing Tubby, but the only thing he could do was to hop up and down and flap his wings.

'Didn't you even see which way he went?' the Lion asked.

'He went through the kitchen window. The Money-Pig saw him.'

'If you say that again,' bellowed the Money-Pig, 'I shall certainly beat you! Someone give me a penny; I am going to be ill!'

'It's all the Easter Chicken's fault!' they shouted in chorus.

In the very midst of this confusion, there was heard the shrill toot of a horn, and a loud ring at the doorbell. Someone must be arriving in style! And while they wondered, the toy-cupboard door was flung open, and in strode Poor Cecco himself, together with Bulka and a strange little person with painted boots and no frock on, whom they had never seen before. She looked very shy, and was carrying a bundle in her hand.

'Hello!' cried Poor Cecco. 'How is everybody? Hello, Harlequin! Hello, Lion! Hello, Anna! This is Jensina. We've been all over the world and now we're back again!' And he began kissing them all round.

'And I've brought some beads for Tubby!' Bulka cried, holding up his necklace for everyone to see. 'Nobody touch them! Where is Tubby?'

All the toys were silent; no one wanted to speak first. Only the Money-Pig was heard to snore loudly.

'Where is Tubby?' Bulka repeated. 'I want to see Tubby! Why isn't Tubby here?'

And Poor Cecco, looking about him, asked with a sudden sternness: 'Where is Tubby?'

The toys looked uneasily one at another, shuffling their feet, and suddenly they all burst into tears.

CHAPTER 15

How Bulka got his letters

HERE was a dismal end to a fine home-coming!

Well the toys might weep; that would not help matters. Poor Cecco's return, however, after the first few moments – in which he said very plainly what he thought – put new courage into them all. Now there was someone to organise the search and take matters in hand, and at once they became brave. The Lion stiffened up and was ready to roar; Anna stopped snivelling, and Harlequin squared his shoulders and went about once more saying 'Hey Presto!' They ceased to blame the Easter Chicken, and instead began to talk of what they would do to Murrum.

The real question, however, was to rescue Tubby, and this could not be done until she was found. Poor Cecco at once decided that they must divide into two parties, one to search the garden and one the house. This, the Lion pointed out, had already been done, but Poor Cecco wanted to make quite sure. So with Poor Cecco at the head of one party, and Bulka leading the other, they set out.

Jensina remained at home, with Ida, Anna and the dolls, in order to become acquainted.

Now I would like nothing better than to tell how Gladys and Virginia May welcomed Jensina with the kindness due to a stranger and a guest, but unfortunately this would not be at all true. In fact, from the first minute they set eyes on Jensina they had made up their minds to snub her. This was partly due to jealousy, partly from the mere desire to show off and give themselves airs. As long as Bulka and Poor Cecco were present they were bound to be polite to her, but as soon as they found themselves alone they turned up their noses and set out to make her just as uncomfortable as they knew how. Anna merely simpered and looked affected. Ida alone was kind, but then Ida was always kind. No one took any notice of *her*.

As for Jensina, the unaccustomed luxury of the toy-cupboard, and the new company among which she found herself, naturally made her feel a little shy. She consoled herself, however, and kept up her sense of dignity by sticking out her tongue whenever Gladys and Virginia May were not looking. She was quite aware of their attitude, and would have much preferred to join Poor Cecco and Bulka on their search, but instead she had to stay at home and make the best of it. So she sat on the toy-cupboard sofa, which had only two legs and was propped up at the other end by an empty cotton-spool, while Gladys and Virginia May reclined on the cigar-box opposite and stared at her.

'Are there many parties where you come from?' Virginia May began in a languid voice.

'There were two last night,' Jensina replied, 'but I could only attend one of them.'

'Indeed!' said Gladys, and the two dolls glanced at one another and sniffed.

'I suppose you have all your clothes in that funny bundle,' Gladys remarked. 'So quaint! I wish, Virginia,' she added, 'that you would remind me to have the lock of my large trunk attended to, I may go visiting soon, and I couldn't dream of travelling without it! I don't quite know whether I shall wear my white satin or the pink velvet trimmed with lace. Harlequin says I look charming in the pink velvet!'

The trunk, as everyone knew, did not really belong to Gladys at all. It had lain in the bottom of the toy-cupboard for ages with the lid half off and was full of broken china, while the white satin petticoat had only been loaned her for the wedding last week, and it was Virginia May's turn to have it next. Virginia, however, chose to forget that she had quarrelled bitterly with Gladys over this garment only two days ago, and clasping her hands she exclaimed:

'Oh, darling, I should wear the white! White is always so becoming when one travels, especially with a veil.'

'I dare say you are right,' sighed Gladys, and she glanced again at Jensina.

'Wouldn't you like to take your shoes off,' she asked sweetly, 'and rest your feet a little?'

Now Jensina couldn't possibly take her shoes off, and both the dolls knew it. They were painted on, and while painted-on shoes are the cheapest and most comfortable that anyone can have, they are also the sign of inferior social position. Both Gladys and Virginia had once possessed real shoes – bronze paper shoes with buckles – but they had been lost long ago, and one of Viginia's feet being broken off near the instep, she couldn't have kept a shoe on even if she still had it; Jensina knew they were only trying to humiliate her, but she didn't care; her feet were both unchipped and they served her quite well for walking. So she merely stared hard at Virginia's broken toes and replied:

'I never take my shoes off in company. I don't think it is quite nice!'

Both dolls turned very red.

'I dare say she sleeps in them,' Virginia whispered in a loud aside, and Gladys returned: 'We might lend her something to wear. Poor thing! I think I've got an old petticoat somewhere about.'

'I've got a perfectly good dress of my own,' Jensina replied aloud, 'and it doesn't need washing either!'

'Really!' said Virginia. 'How strange! What is it made of?'

'It's made of gingham,' said Jensina proudly.

'Gingham!' murmured the dolls, and they both shuddered.

'Don't you mind them,' whispered Ida kindly. 'They're only jealous because you've travelled more than they have. They're quite nice when you really know them.'

'They're stuck-up cats!' thought Jensina. '*That's* what they are!'

She sat stiff and erect on the sofa, determined to keep silence, while the two dolls plied her with questions. They were curious, above all, to know what kind of a shop she came from.

'I was never in a shop,' Jensina retorted at last. 'My people had nothing to do with trade. If you want to know, I am descended from a gypsy queen!'

'Descended is the right word!' said Virginia, while Gladys added: 'I never knew there were gypsy queens.'

'Then you don't know much,' said Jensina sharply, and turning her back on them as far as she could she began to unknot her bundle and arrange its contents on the sofa beside her, while Virginia and Gladys stared inquisitively, whispering together.

'It must be very romantic being a queen!' simpered Anna coyly, thinking of the Lion. It was the first remark she had made and Jensina turned to stare at her.

'Why do you wear that bell round your neck?' she asked.

'In case I ever get lost,' Anna replied, 'so that I can always tell where I am, even in the dark.'

'I shouldn't think *you'd* get lost easily!' said Jensina.

Anna did not know whether this was a compliment or not, so she merely simpered again. Jensina went on arranging her treasures, which made the dolls very curious, and Gladys leaned so far over Virginia May's shoulder that they both lost their balance and tumbled off the cigar-box. To hide their confusion Gladys said instantly:

'Let us have a little music! Anna, will you find the musical-box?'

This took Anna some while, partly because her eyes were so near the top of her head, partly because the musical-box itself was hidden under a pile of broken furniture and building blocks in one corner of the toy-cupboard. While she was still looking for it Bulka came in, followed by the Lion and the Easter Chicken.

'Have you found Tubby?' the others cried at once. 'Have you any news?'

'Not yet,' replied the Lion hopefully, 'but Poor Cecco and Harlequin are in the garden making a trap, and if only Murrum will step on it we might catch him.'

'Have you had a nice time, Jensina?' Bulka asked.

'Wonderful!' replied Jensina, looking straight at the two dolls, who became more confused than ever. Anna had found the musical-box at last. It was round, with painted figures on it and a tiny china knob on the handle. Seizing this she began to turn, and immediately a little tune gushed forth.

'Tum tum tum tumptity – ugh – ugh – ugh!' tinkled the musical-box, breaking off, as always, in something between a cough and a hiccup.

At the sound of these familiar strains, to which he and Tubby had so often waltzed in bygone days, Poor Bulka nearly broke down. 'Stop it!' he cried, stamping his foot. 'Stop it!' while Anna gazed in stupid surprise and the musical-box, which was far harder to stop than to set going, continued obstinately in its refrain.

'Stop it!' shouted the Money-Pig, aroused from his nap on the roof of the Noah's Ark. '*Must* you make that horrible noise?'

Jensina rushed to take hold of the handle, and as she did so the Money-Pig, leaning over to shout, caught sight of the penny – Poor Cecco's remaining penny – lying with Jensina's treasures on the toy-cupboard sofa.

'There's money!' he exclaimed. 'I see it! Give it me at once!'

'I shall not,' returned Jensina with spirit. 'It belongs to Poor Cecco!'

'He can't take care of money! I need it! Give it me this instant!' the Money-Pig insisted. 'No one can have money but me!'

'Don't you give it him!' advised the Lion. 'You'll never get it back. He's awfully greedy!'

Jensina, who had no intention of giving up the penny, took a step back, startled by the Money-Pig's squealing, while the Easter Chicken suddenly piped up: 'I'll find you a penny if you'll tell that you saw Murrum stealing Tubby!'

'I won't!' the Money-Pig bellowed. 'I won't tell you! Give me that penny at once!'

It all happened in a moment! Jensina made a movement to protect Poor Cecco's money, snatching it from the sofa; the Money-Pig gave a shriek, and in his rage he leaned so far forward that his hoof slipped, he lost his balance, and – crash! – he fell off the Noah's Ark roof and was broken to pieces!

There he lay in fragments on the toy-cupboard floor, and there, among the pennies, and the scraps of green china that a moment ago had been his ears and his snout and his fat bulging sides, lay dozens and dozens of folded notes of all shapes and sizes – a whole pile of them – each one addressed: 'To Dear Bulka. In the Toy-Cupboard.' – all Tubby's love letters that she had written so carefully and posted inside him! The wonder was that he had held them all up to now without bursting!

There they were, plain for all the world to see, with 'Dear Bulka' written in a big round hand on each one of them. 'Tubby's been writing to me! Tubby's written me a letter!' Bulka cried. He began to gather the letters up in armfuls, dropping half of them in his haste.

'Hurry up and open them!' said Jensina. 'Perhaps they're to tell us where she is.'

'What's this?' asked Poor Cecco, coming in from the garden, with Harlequin at his heels. 'What's happened?'

Bulka had torn open one of the letters, and there he read:

> 'DEAR BULKA:
>
> I love you more than everything and I will make you a big cake with ammons and Icing and Silver balls,
>
> Your loving
>
> TUBBY.
>
> P.S. There will be candels on the Cake.

'Tubby loves me!' Bulka shouted, waving the letter over his head. 'Tubby really loves me! She wrote it down!'

'Show us!' cried the dolls instantly.

'Indeed I won't!' said Bulka. 'It's only written for me, so Hinksman!' And gathering all his letters together – an enormous armful – he hastened off to read them all alone by himself in the garden.

Jensina looked down at the green fragments that had lately been the Money-Pig.

'Do you suppose he's dead?' she asked Poor Cecco in an awed voice.

'Very likely,' returned Poor Cecco. 'If he is we'll have a funeral, but there's no time to see about that now. Come out, Jensina, and I'll show you my trap!'

Ida was the only one who felt sorry for the Money-Pig. Not that she liked him – no one had done that – but she had a naturally soft heart, even for disagreeable people. So she set about sweeping him up, as well as she could, and put all the best pieces in the doll's trunk to wait till there was time for a funeral.

She had just brushed up the last chip when Gladys, who had wandered off and climbed up to the front window to look out, returned in great excitement.

'Anna – Ida!' Gladys exclaimed. 'What *do* you think? I just looked out of the window, and there are two enormous grey rats sitting behind the flower-pot on the front porch!'

CHAPTER 16

In the willow tree

IT'S really time, now, that we heard something about Tubby herself.

Luckily Tubby was very soft, so when Murrum dropped her down the hole in the willow tree she only bounced a little, and didn't hurt herself at all.

When her first fright was over, and she was able to look about her, she found that she was in a large round room with very high walls. There was a pale greenish light in the place, which came from the decayed wood with which the inside of the willow tree was lined, and which shone in the dark; everything looked very clean and nice, and there was a soft thick carpet of earth and wood-dust underfoot. High up, through the hole in the top, she could see a big bright star.

In fact, if Tubby had found this place for herself, instead of being thrown into it so rudely by Murrum, she would have asked for nothing better. All her life she had wanted a house of her own, and had she been free to choose, this was just such a house as she would have chosen. Certainly there was the fear that Murrum might come back, but there seemed no danger of that for the present. For the rest, it was as roomy as the toy-cupboard and far more tidy. If Bulka were only here to play with her, Tubby thought, they could have a wonderful time; and thinking of Bulka she remembered the unfinished letter and the pencil which she had thrust hastily into her pocket when Murrum seized her.

Taking it out, she sat down with her back against the wall, licked the point of her pencil well, and began to write:

> DEAR BULKA:
>
> I am in a funny place it is a house in a tree. Murrum brought me it is lited with green lites so no more at present. Hoping you are well your loving
>
> TUBBY.
>
> P.S. I will make you a cake with ammons and Icing and Silver balls.

When she had finished writing Tubby walked round and round the room looking for a place to post her letter, but she could see no crack or cranny large enough, and the walls looked exactly the same all round. So at last she gave it up, and feeling somewhat dizzy from walking in a circle so long she cuddled down in a hollow in the floor and shut her eyes.

When she awoke it was daylight, and the sun was shining in through the hole in the top of the tree. Tubby could see blue sky, with silver-green willow leaves waving before it, high above her. Little ants were running up and down the willow tree walls. She sat up and began to feel very hungry.

Suddenly there was a whirr of wings, and a spotted woodpecker with a scarlet head flew down inside the tree. He looked very astonished.

'Hallo!' he exclaimed. 'Where did you come from?'

'I come from Tubbyland,' said Tubby instantly, 'and I would like some breakfast.'

'Tubbyland –' said the woodpecker, clinging upside-down to the wall in a way that made Tubby dizzy to look at. 'Hm. I don't know where that is! And as for breakfast, I've enough to do getting that for my own family, but if there's any left over you shall have it.'

He flew off, as good as his word, and in a few minutes he was back again but the breakfast he brought was not at all what Tubby had hoped for. It was a great fat worm, squirmy and unpleasant, and he dropped it so nearly into Tubby's mouth, as she sat looking up, that she gave a little scream. He was off again instantly, and to hide her disappointment, and not to hurt the woodpecker's feelings, she buried the worm as quickly as she could under the loose earth on the floor, where she would not be obliged to see it.

She had only just finished, and was scraping the earth together again, when – bang – something hit her right on the nose. This time it was a nut, neatly cracked, so that Tubby had no trouble at all in getting the kernel out and eating it. It belonged to a squirrel, who was watching Tubby so intently that he let his nut fall without meaning to.

Whirr! The woodpecker was back again, and with another worm, even fatter and squirmier than the first, dangling from his bill.

'Open your mouth!' he called cheerfully.

'I've had plenty!' Tubby cried. 'Indeed I have! Please don't trouble any more!'

'Nonsense!' said the woodpecker. 'Young people must eat. I don't know where you come from, but we'll see to it that you don't starve. The children send this with their love!'

And he dropped the worm plop into her lap.

Luckily he didn't wait to see what became of it.

'I hate breakfast!' thought Tubby. For one worm after another, every few minutes, came tumbling down on her head. It kept her busy burying them all, and even then their tails would come wriggling up again, in a way that was most unpleasant. But presently, to her relief, the supply of worms gave out, or else the woodpecker thought she had had enough, for he ceased to appear, and Tubby was just shovelling the earth over the last and biggest worm of all when a voice overhead said:

'What are you doing down there?'

Tubby looked up. She was getting a crick in her neck from having to tilt her head back so often. This time it was the squirrel again.

'None of your business!' cried Tubby, for she was afraid he would tell the woodpecker. 'I'm tidying my house,' she added with dignity.

'Are you the new Janitor?'

'Indeed I'm not,' Tubby replied.

'Then I don't know why you are here,' said the squirrel. 'You look like some kind of an orphan. Why did you eat my nut?'

'I was hungry,' said Tubby. 'I thought it was meant for me.'

'Never mind,' the squirrel said. 'Plenty more where that came from.' And he slapped his pocket. 'I'll come down and talk to you, if you like.'

He came skipping down the side of the wall and dropped neatly to the floor, where he sat watching her with his bright beady eyes.

'This basement isn't so bad,' he remarked presently, 'if you were to fix it up a little. Myself, I always prefer living in the upper story. But perhaps you had no choice.'

'Indeed I hadn't,' thought Tubby, but she didn't tell the squirrel so. Instead she kept silence, and merely occupied herself with walking round and round the room, staring hard at the grey walls and humming as she did so, till at last the squirrel exclaimed: 'Don't do that! It makes me giddy! What are you looking for?'

'I'm looking for a place to post my letter,' Tubby explained.

'Oh, I thought you might be looking for a job,' said the squirrel, 'and you certainly won't find one there. Can you read and write?'

'Of course!' said Tubby proudly.

'Then stop poking your fingers into those cracks and listen to me. I've got three children at home. They're smaller than you, but about the same colour. That's why I thought you might be an orphan. Do you want to come and teach them?'

'Teach them what?' Tubby asked.

'Anything you like,' said the squirrel, waving his tail vaguely.

Tubby thought a little while.

'I'd like to see the house first,' she said.

'It's just up there,' said the squirrel. Looking up, Tubby saw for the first time a big hole half-way up the wall of the tree, which she had not noticed the night before.

'How do you get up?' she asked.

'This way,' said the squirrel, and he ran up and down the wall two or three times, clinging with his claws and making a funny scratchy sound as he went.

'I can't do that!' Tubby said.

'I'll help you,' said the squirrel. And he did, pushing her from behind and showing her where to put her paws.

It was easier than she expected. 'If he can help me so far,' Tubby thought, 'he might be able to help me right up to the top.' But first she wanted to see the squirrels' home.

It was in a hollow limb of the tree, that reached a long way back like a passage. It was stuffy in there and very warm, and it smelled of fur and hay and nutshells; either the squirrels ate all their meals in the bedroom or else they slept in the pantry. Tubby could not quite make up her mind which. But the sight of the baby squirrels, sitting up in bed with their little paws clasped and their round eyes gazing up at her, pleased her so much that she sat down then and there among the hay and nutshells and took them all three on her lap.

'We want a story!' cried the baby squirrels. 'Tell us a story!'

Tubby began immediately:

'Once there was a little mouse and he lived in Tubbyland and he wore blue trousers, and one day he said to his mother, "Mother, I would like a party!" "Very well," said his mother, "you have been a good child," and she took him down a *long* passage and opened the door, and there was a Christmas tree with candles on it and shiny lights—'

'I want to go down the passage!' cried the three baby squirrels all at once, and they began to jump up and down.

'Wait a minute,' said Tubby. 'I haven't told you what they had to eat at the party, yet.'

'What had to eat?' asked the baby squirrels, clasping their paws.

Tubby went on hurriedly: 'They had all kinds of cake and biscuits, and carrots and nuts and peppermint, and a great be-*yoo*tiful cake with orange icing and silver balls on it, and three candles—'

'Want some nuts!' the baby squirrels began again. 'Want some nuts!'

'Don't be little pigs!' said Tubby severely, for she didn't like being interrupted. 'How can I tell you stories if you jump up and down all the time? So they lived happily ever after,' she finished in a loud firm voice. 'And now one of you find me the comb and I'll comb your hair.'

After much hunting the baby squirrels found the comb under the bedclothes, and Tubby set about making them tidy. This was a task she thoroughly enjoyed; their hair was so soft and silky and parted so perfectly down the back, and it was such fun to comb out those long feathery tails till they shone like spun glass. The only trouble was that as soon as she finished one squirrel and set him aside, he at once began bouncing about in the hay and made himself all untidy again, until Tubby was almost in despair.

'Were there ever such wriggly children!' she exclaimed. 'Be quiet, do!' And she sat the last squirrel down very hard, hoping that he would stay this time, for she wanted to explore the rest of the house.

Beyond the squirrels' living-room the passage grew very narrow, so Tubby had hard work to squeeze herself along. It began to smell

musty and wormy, too; evidently no one had used it for a long while. But Tubby wriggled on, for she was bound to see what lay at the end.

Soon it grew lighter. There was a small knothole in the wall, near the end of the passage, and as soon as Tubby caught sight of this she thought: 'Now I can post my letter at last!' And pulling the letter from her pocket she poked it through the knothole and let it fall.

As she turned round she bumped against something sharp. It was the corner of a box that had been pushed into a hollow right at the end of the passage. It was wedged there so tightly, covered over with dust and cobwebs, that Tubby had difficulty in pulling it out. But she managed it at last, and saw scratched on the lid the initials T.L.

'That's for Tubbyland,' thought Tubby. 'Perhaps there are chocolates in!' And lifting up the lid she looked inside.

There were no chocolates in, but there was something far more interesting. There was, first of all, a gold thimble, and then a silver dime with a hole in it, and a bit of tinsel and some red worsted, and a ring with a bright green stone, and a bit of broken looking-glass and three safety-pins and a gilt watch and chain, just the right size for Poor Cecco. And when she had pulled all these things out, there, folded away at the bottom, under some scraps of coloured paper and silk, was a brand-new red velvet coat with gold buttons, and a little pair of sky-blue trousers trimmed with silver braid!

They might have been made to the very measure of Bulka!

Tubby's paws shook with excitement as she folded the clothes up again and tumbled everything back into the box. She could hear footsteps along the passage. It was the squirrel, come back to see how she was getting along.

'Look what I found!' cried Tubby. 'Look what I found! There's T.L. on it. It came from Tubbyland!'

'That's a queer thing!' said the squirrel, peering into the box with his head on one side. 'That must have belonged to old Miss Magpie. She rented this house before we had it, and from what I hear she was a terrible old miser. All sorts of things she had, stored away, and they do say she didn't come by the half of them honestly, either. I wouldn't be at all surprised if she stole these! Anyway you're welcome to them if they're any use to you, for I'm sure I don't want the house cluttered up.'

And while Tubby held her pinafore out he very obligingly stowed everything into it, the box being too big to carry.

That evening, after she had tucked the baby squirrels into bed, tidied up the nutshells, and bidden Mr Squirrel good-night, Tubby sat on the floor at the bottom of the tree, with her treasures spread about her. She unfolded the little coat and trousers, folded them again, laid them in every possible position to see how beautiful they looked. How pleased Bulka would be! How fine he would look with these elegant blue trousers on, and the red coat buttoned down the front!

Oh, why wasn't Bulka here!

A great tear rolled down and splashed on the blue velvet. Anxiously Tubby wiped it off with the hem of her pinafore, but it was no use; another fell, and another — She pushed the clothes aside and sat very still, blinking hard.

Dusk fell; the walls about her shone once more with their soft greenish light. Poor Tubby felt very lonely and very homesick. Never had she missed Bulka so much. She groped in her pocket for the pencil. There was just one tiny scrap of paper left, all crumpled, and smoothing it out she tried to write. But the words wouldn't come, and the pencil danced up and down before her eyes.

Suddenly, on the outside wall of the tree she heard, very faint and far off, a tiny tapping!

CHAPTER 17

The letter from the sky

'YOU see,' explained Poor Cecco, 'if Murrum happens to walk by here, and if he only happens to put his paw on that piece of wood, then this will pull that, and that *this* – and then the whole stick will fall down right on his back!'

'A lot of good that will do!' said Jensina.

They were in the garden, by the onion bed, looking at the trap which Poor Cecco had invented, while Harlequin stood by, well pleased with his share in the work.

'Anyway it will give him a good fright,' Poor Cecco retorted.

'Why did you put it here?' Jensina objected. 'Murrum doesn't eat onions, does he?'

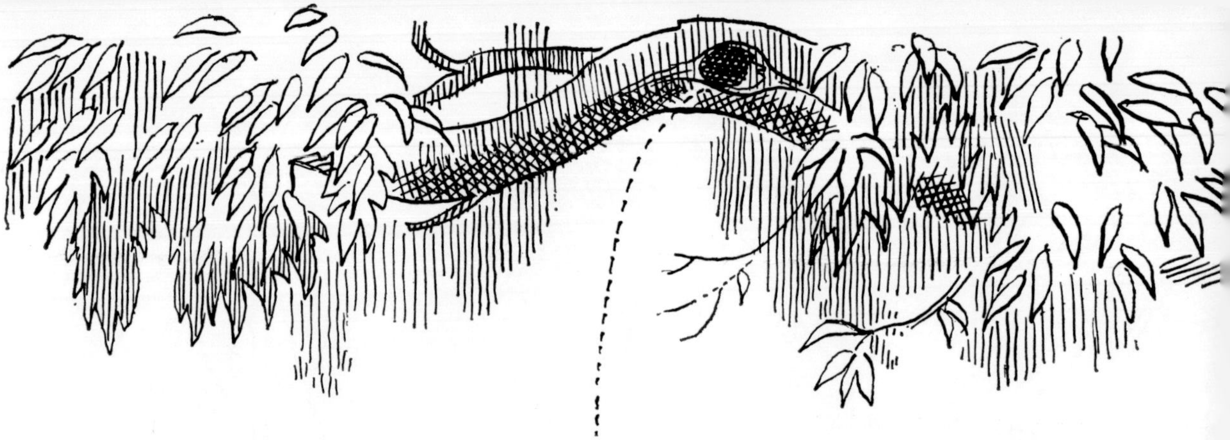

'Because it's the only place where the earth is soft enough. You don't seem to understand, Jensina,' he went on indignantly, 'that it took *ages* digging that hole out!'

'I've known a lot of cats,' Jensina remarked, 'but I've only known one that was an idiot, and *he* got drowned in the buttermilk pail!'

'I wonder where Bulka is?' said Poor Cecco after a moment, wishing to change the conversation.

'I thought I heard him calling a minute ago,' Harlequin replied. 'Look, there he comes!' And he pointed down the garden path.

Bulka, when he left the house, had, after some search for a quiet nook, settled down with his armful of letters under the shade of a rhubarb plant. The rhubarb stems were tall; the broad leaves spread out like a tent, and beneath their shelter he felt secure from prying

eyes. Spreading the letters out, he read them all through, one by one, and as he read his little heart trembled with emotion. Dear Tubby, what beautiful things she had written here and all for him alone!

He couldn't sit still any longer; he must jump up and wander about in the sunshine and think of it all. With the precious letters, tied all together by a strong grass-blade, clutched close to his heart, he skipped along, up one border and down the next, paying no particular attention to where he was going and only thinking of his dear Tubby, when, just as he paused to give an extra skip and wriggle – ping! – something fell right on the top of his head!

It was the very letter which Tubby, as you will remember, had posted through the hole in the willow tree branch!

Certainly that letter had lost no time on the way.

Bulka rubbed his head, looked up at the green branches above him, down at the ground, and saw the letter lying there, addressed to him, on the garden path. His first thought was that it had somehow dropped from the packet in his arms. But no, the grass band was still unbroken; nothing was missing.

He opened the letter and read:

> DEAR BULKA:
>
> I am in a funny place it is a house in a tree Murrum brought me It is lited with green lites—

When he had read as far as this Bulka started off at a run, across the herb borders, through the marigold thicket, up one path and down the next, calling loudly for Poor Cecco and Harlequin.

'I've got a letter from Tubby!' he cried breathlessly, when at last he caught sight of Harlequin's head above the onion tops.

'We know,' Jensina said. 'You told us. Goodness, Bulka, you're out of breath!'

'It's a new letter,' he told them. 'It fell out of the sky!'

'Show me!' said Poor Cecco. And he read it aloud.

Plainly, if the letter were true, Tubby was in a tree. But which tree? They looked round. The whole garden was full of trees.

'Where did you find it?' Poor Cecco asked.

Bulka thought, staring about him, and his face grew doubtful. 'I don't know,' he said at last. 'It just fell on me.'

'But surely you remember? Where were you walking?'

'I was walking – I was walking everywhere!' said Bulka. Which was very nearly true. 'I'd been all over the garden, and then it fell on me, and I ran – and I ran, and I couldn't find you!'

'*I* call that silly!' said Jensina.

But Poor Cecco, seeing that Bulka was very near to tears – a thing that had not happened for a long time, for during his travels he had learned to be quite brave – said kindly: 'Never mind, Bulka! Tubby's in a tree, that we know, and we'll hunt the garden over till we find her, if it takes us all night!'

All the others came running when they heard the glad news – even the Express Wagon rumbled along, in case he should be needed on ambulance duty – and together they set out to search the garden from end to end.

It took them a long while. They began with the smallest trees first – like the rose trees – because they were the easiest. Some of them were so small that it would hardly have been possible for the Easter Chicken, let alone Tubby, to have been hidden in them, but as Poor Cecco said, it was best to leave nothing untried. So at each one they peered and tapped and listened.

There was some discussion between Harlequin and the Wooden Engine as to whether the raspberry canes were trees or flowers, but this Poor Cecco decided. He said they were vegetables. While they ran to and fro among the garden beds the Express Wagon kept pace with them, as nearly as he could, on the path.

They all worked with a will. Anna got tangled in a fallen pea-vine. Bulka scratched himself in the currant bushes, but still they kept on, tapping and calling, till gradually the sun sank lower and the shadows began to lengthen.

It was nearly dusk when they found themselves, thoroughly disheartened, in the corner beyond the parsley bed. Suddenly Anna, whose upturned eyes were invaluable in a search of this kind, exclaimed:

'Isn't that a tree?'

It was the willow, its huge grey trunk looming above them, grey and enormous. It was so big to their eyes that none of them before had even thought of it as a tree at all. Now, at Anna's remark, they looked up. Certainly there were branches on it, and sprays of green leaves here and there.

'It's a mountain,' said the Engine.

'No,' said Poor Cecco, 'it is a tree. It has bark. But it is a much too large tree.'

'Do you suppose Tubby's *there*?' Gladys whispered, overawed.

Bulka's heart sank at the thought of Tubby, shut up in that enormous fortress. But he rushed up and began to pound on the rough grey bark.

There was no answer.

'We must try all the way round,' Poor Cecco said.

So all the way round they walked, tapping and listening. Suddenly Bulka, who had his ear glued to the trunk, cried, 'Listen, all of you! I hear something!'

Instantly they all stood still. Somewhere within the tree could be heard a distinct answering tap.

'It's Tubby!' cried Bulka. 'It's Tubby! Tubby,' he called, 'is that you?'

Quite clearly he heard the tiny voice:

'Yes, Bulka!'

'Where are you, Tubby?' he asked.

And again the tiny voice whispered back:

'In Tubbyland, Bulka!'

'I told you!' said Gladys triumphantly. 'I told you all along that's where she was. Now at any rate we know where that wretched Tubby-land is!'

But the others paid no heed. They all had their ears to the tree – except naturally the Wooden Engine, who kept exclaiming: 'What is she saying? What does she say?' and hopping up and down on his wheels with excitement.

'How can we get her out?' Harlequin asked.

How indeed? In vain they walked round and round the tree; there was no sign of a door anywhere, and of course they knew nothing of the hole in the top.

'We might tunnel underneath,' Poor Cecco said. And he began to dig, but his paws soon came against the hard roots, and he was forced to stop.

'Maybe she'll eat her way out!' suggested the Lion hopefully.

No one thought this very likely. Harlequin stared at the tree, saying, 'Hey Presto!' but as usual with no result.

'At any rate,' said Poor Cecco, 'we won't desert her!'

'We'll stay by the tree all night!' declared the Lion.

And this they prepared to do, each at his station, leaning with their backs against the tree, while the Engine and the Express Wagon parked themselves side by side, within easy call, at the edge of the path.

Night fell; the moon shone out; every few minutes Bulka could be heard whispering: 'Tubby, are you asleep? Good night, Tubby!'

And in the branches above them a black form crouched, sleek and still. It was Murrum, thoroughly well pleased with his performance. There he sat, and stared down with pale contemptuous eyes on the faithful watchers gathered round the tree.

CHAPTER 18

The rescue

PRESENTLY Poor Cecco felt someone nudging him. It was Jensina, who had crept softly round from the other side of the tree.

'Listen,' she whispered. 'Listen, I have an idea!'

'What is it?' Poor Cecco whispered back.

Jensina, standing there on tiptoe, looked strangely excited. Her eyes shone in the moonlight.

'You know the rats? Do you remember what the Iron Grenadier said? Oh, Poor Cecco, suppose we get the rats to gnaw the tree and let Tubby out?'

'Jensina!' he exclaimed. 'It's wonderful! But they could never gnaw this tree through!'

'Rats can do anything,' Jensina said.

'They aren't here.'

'They are. Sh-sh! I never told you, but Gladys saw them. The Easter Chicken told me. They are sitting on the front porch.'

'Have you got the Tooth?'

'It's here,' said Jensina. 'I didn't dare leave it in the house.' She showed him the mysterious object, in its silver-paper wrapping. Poor Cecco gazed at it for a moment in silence.

'Oh, Jensina, aren't you afraid? Let me go!' he entreated.

'No,' replied Jensina firmly. 'I took the Tooth, and it's I who must bargain with them. But you may keep quite near me,' she added.

Brave as she was, Jensina's heart went thump – thump, as she advanced along the path towards the house. Hastily Poor Cecco had warned the others of her plan, and while he walked beside her they followed in a body, clinging to one another for protection, yet thrilled with curiosity to see what was going to happen.

And now they had reached the last patch of open moonlight between the lilac bush and the dark shadow of the porch. Here Jensina paused, while Poor Cecco whispered his last entreaties.

'Now, do be careful, Jensina! Remember what the Grenadier told you. Make them promise everything first, and *don't* make a muddle of it!'

'Do you think I'm an idiot?' she demanded.

These words, so characteristic of Jensina's brave spirit, did much to restore his confidence. He stood back, as she bade him, and alone Jensina strode forth into the patch of moonlight.

Immediately, from the porch shadow, the two rats came forward to meet her. Poor Cecco and Bulka recognised them at once; they were the two policemen rats who had followed them all along. They looked bigger and fiercer than ever. On they came, their whiskers twitching, their hind legs stretched behind, and within a few inches of Jensina they paused, sat up, and waited.

Jensina began to speak in the rat language, slowly at first, and then more rapidly. The rats nodded. Jensina pointed down the garden. The rats nodded again. She raised her hand, and the watchers could see distinctly the silver-paper shining in the moonlight.

The rats saw it too; one of them took a step forward, but with a swift gesture Jensina warned him back. Still holding the Tooth, she repeated, very slowly and distinctly, every word that she had said before, pausing every now and then to think whether she had left anything out.

The rats nodded once more, and now their faces were pleased and friendly. The fattest rat bowed. Then, while Poor Cecco fairly held his breath with suspense he came forward, and stretching out his paw politely took from Jensina's hand the Tooth. Placing it in his mouth, he made one leap, and where he went does not matter, for he vanishes from this story for ever, and the tooth with him.

Instantly there was a scuffling and squeaking. From every bush, from every patch of shadow, rats appeared. Grey rats, brown rats, old and young, dozens and dozens of them. Bulka gave a squeal of fright, but this time the rats paid no attention to him. Straight down the garden path they poured, scattering the toys in their course, over the parsley bed, right to the old willow, and by the time the toys had pulled themselves together and hurried back, they were already hard at work gnawing a hole in the side of the tree.

'Look!' Jensina cried, clapping her hand. 'They're cutting a doorway! Aren't they clever? I told you they could do anything!'

The rats were in fact working in a circle, clinging with their feet to the bark while they gnawed. Soon the sawdust began to fall in a powdery heap that grew rapidly larger.

'Jensina!' Bulka cried. 'How can I ever thank you!'

Jensina indeed was the heroine of the moment. Even the dolls smiled and tried to make up for the mean way they had acted. How they had misjudged her! If only, Gladys thought, she had known beforehand what an important person Jensina really was!

Meantime Anna, always timid, had been so alarmed by the sudden flood of rats that she ran away up the side path, straight towards the onion bed. Staring up at the sky as always, she never saw Poor Cecco's trap until she had stumbled right on it. The stick came down with a whack, one corner of Anna's green meadow sank into the hole Poor Cecco had so carefully dug, and stuck fast; there she stayed, tilted perilously sidewise, snivelling with fear and pain and ringing her bell loudly for help.

This time the Lion heard her. For all that he was a Lion, the nearness of those rats, and their long white teeth, made him strangely uncomfortable inside, and he was only too glad of any excuse to move away.

Tenderly he helped Anna out of the pit, and dried her tears, and together they stood in the moonlight side by side.

'If you would only flee with me to the jungle, dear Anna,' the Lion murmured for the hundred and first time, 'this sort of thing wouldn't happen!'

'I'm always fleeing,' returned Anna pettishly, for her back still smarted where the stick had hit it, 'and look what comes of it! Even my green meadow is no longer safe nowadays! Not but what one might as well *be* in the jungle and have done with it,' she added rather more graciously, 'with all those nasty rats about!'

And bending her head to simper at the Lion, she released it rather too suddenly, producing a loud and prolonged 'baa-a-a!' which startled even herself.

'Your voice is like music,' the Lion whispered, gazing at her adoringly.

And Anna simpered again.

The carpenter rats had worked so hard that by now they had nearly bitten through the tree. The toys stood round, breathless with excitement, while the sawdust fell faster and faster, and at last the section of bark, round which they had been gnawing, began to tremble.

Bulka, who had disappeared, came running up, carrying the blue beads which he had just fetched from the toy-cupboard.

And now the rats stopped working, wiped their foreheads, and drew back. The leader, clinging with his paws, gave one last bite, and the bark fell outwards, leaving a neat arched doorway through which, after a moment's hushed suspense, Tubby herself walked proudly forth, bearing in one paw the scarlet jacket and in the other the sky-blue trousers trimmed with braid.

'Bulka!' cried Tubby.

'Tubby!' cried Bulka.

And they fell in each other's arms.

The leader of the rats came up to Jensina, holding out a folded yellow paper which he drew from his breast pocket.

'Sign on the dotted line, please!' he said.

She wrote her name in large letters: JENSINA.

'Thank you,' said the rat, glancing at it. 'And if you ever need another little job done, remember we give prompt service and are always willing to oblige.'

The second policeman rat also came forward and shook hands.

'A fine run you give us, young lady,' he said, 'but we don't hold no grudge for that, now that all's friendly-like between us, as you may say. So bygones is bygones, and here's wishing you and the young gentleman every happiness!'

Jensina glanced hastily at Poor Cecco, but he had not heard; he was talking to Tubby.

'Thank you very much!' she said. 'But you are quite mistaken; we are not even engaged!'

'Well, you never know your luck!' returned the rat, smiling broadly, and he touched his forehead and moved away.

Harlequin gave a sudden cry: 'There's Murrum!'

Murrum was still crouched on the limb above them, gazing down in fury and switching his tail. It was this black tip, moving in the moonlight, which had caught Harlequin's eye.

'Aha!' cried the rats. 'We'll soon settle that!'

And with a mighty whoop they began to scamper up the willow trunk. Murrum did not wait to meet them; he dropped to the ground, his ears laid back and his fur bristling, and made off over the parsley bed, the rats in glad pursuit.

'They can't really hurt him,' said Jensina. 'They only want to give him a good fright.'

Bulka had hung the blue beads solemnly round Tubby's neck. He stood now, beaming with happiness, while she carefully measured the little jacket and trousers against him. They were exactly right!

'Oh, Tubby!' he whispered. 'Where did you get these lovely clothes?'

'Aren't they nice?' she returned proudly. 'I bought them in Tubby-land!'

CHAPTER 19

The Wedding

AND now, of course, there must be a wedding, and – of course – the wedding must take place in Willow Tree Hall, where, after the ceremony, a grand ball and reception would be held in honour of the bride and bridegroom.

Great preparations were afoot. Bulka's costume was already provided; Tubby, by rights, should wear the white satin petticoat and veil, but Gladys had used the petticoat for so long that it was quite shabby, though the veil might yet pass muster, after being washed and mended, and the spray of orange blossom attached to it was still quite good.

So the dolls and Jensina sewed Tubby a new frock out of the pieces of coloured silk that had been in the Tubbyland box. It had purple sleeves and a bit of pink down the front and was trimmed with tinsel lace. With it she wore the blue beads.

Poor Cecco, who was to give Tubby away, wore a green ribbon tied round his middle, and the gilt watch and chain, a present from the bride.

Virginia May, Gladys and Jensina were bridesmaids, with white ribbons and bouquets of wild parsley blossom.

The wedding gifts were laid out on the cigar-box, covered with a blue cloth.

Jensina gave her drinking cup and the green glass stopper; Poor Cecco his penny. Gladys gave her last year's straw hat, retrimmed, Virginia May a hair-ribbon for Tubby's ears, and the Easter Chicken got up early and picked a large bunch of flowers. Harlequin gave a striped pebble that had been in a brooch. Anna, the Engine and the Lion gave a saucepan, three spoons and a bent napkin-ring, wrapped up in paper. They really belonged in the toy-cupboard, but everyone was delighted that Tubby should have them. The rats presented a blue egg-cup, slightly chipped, an almost new tea-strainer and a silver pencil, sent all the way from the ash-heap country by Rat Express, and the house-mice, to show their gratitude to the toys for driving Murrum away, brought seven thimblefuls of rice, a perfectly good cheese rind and a long pin with a pink head, which they had found under the floorboards.

And now the happy moment had arrived. The Express Wagon, making a fine clatter, drove up with the guests. Harlequin stood ready, the musical-box was all wound up to play; Tubby, in her veil and orange blossoms, and Bulka with his little scarlet coat and sky-blue trousers, were just about to kneel down side by side upon Ida, who had begged this privilege—

But they didn't. They couldn't, because Ida wasn't there. And on enquiry, it appeared that no one had seen Ida since the early morning. Without Ida the wedding could not very well proceed, but just as they were all getting quite concerned the Easter Chicken called out:

'Here's Ida! And, my goodness, look what she's bringing!'

Ida, with her tender heart, had felt really upset when she saw the

OVER THE
AVES

'Hey Presto!" and immediately they were married.

Money-Pig in pieces on the floor. All through the day, at intervals, she thought of him, put tidily away in the doll's trunk. And now, when Tubby was found again and everyone so happy it seemed too bad the Money-Pig, unpopular as he was, should be missing all the good times.

So after much hunting about Ida found an old tube of glue in a box on the pantry floor, and very secretly, while the others were busy, she set herself down in a corner of the toy-cupboard beside the doll's trunk and proceeded to glue him together. It was a hard job; many of the pieces were chipped and wouldn't fit, one ear was lost entirely, though Ida searched high and low for it; but in the end she got him together somehow, and more or less like his former self, except that the slit in his back would always remain a little crooked, try as she might. Well pleased with her labour, she had to wait till the glue was dry enough for him to be moved, and he could be brought, with the help of the Wooden Engine, as far as the Willow Tree. So there he stood at last, rather patchy in parts, shaky still on his legs and not a little ashamed of himself – but ravenously hungry.

Hurrying forward with many apologies Ida laid herself on the ground. Tubby and Bulka knelt down on her, side by side. In a hushed silence Bulka took the ring with the green stone and slipped it over Tubby's paw, where it fitted easily. The musical-box burst out with a triumphant 'Tum tum tum tumptity!' Harlequin waved his wand above them, saying 'Hey Presto!' and immediately they were married.

Scarcely was the ceremony over, and everyone had crowded round to kiss the bride, than the Lion came forward, with Anna sidling along behind. They too wanted to get married, seeing how simple it all was. Harlequin was willing, but Poor Cecco put his foot down.

'Nonsense!' he declared. 'One wedding at a time! It's Tubby's turn today, and besides, there are no more gifts ready. Anna has spent all the summer shilly-shallying on account of that stupid green meadow of hers, and now she must just content herself with being engaged for the present!'

So they were engaged, formally; Anna, after some coyness, consented to wear a grass ring round her left ankle, and she took off her bell and hung it about the Lion's neck.

'You were quite right,' Gladys whispered to Poor Cecco. 'Anna could have made up her mind long ago, if she had had any sense.'

That night there was a grand ball in the Willow Tree.

The walls were hung with garlands of flowers; refreshments were set out, and the squirrel arrived, bringing a whole bag of nuts. In the middle stood Tubby's wedding-cake, with Icing AND Almonds AND Silver Balls. And at least three candles. The Toad, with a white apron over his spotted vest, acted as waiter and handed the plates. The three baby squirrels, too small to take part, were allowed to look on from their window until ten o'clock. Everyone wore their best, and in addition to the Musical-box the Grasshopper and Crickets' Jazz Band was engaged to play the dance music.

Never had there been such a gathering; the mice had been busy all morning carrying invitations, and the guests came from far and near.

Softly the green light shone out from the old willow tree walls, making the whole scene beautiful. Tubby danced with Bulka, Jensina and Poor Cecco, Gladys with Harlequin. Anna lumbered, giggling, through a quadrille with the Lion and the Engine – all found partners, and every little while Bulka would break away from the dance and turn somersaults for pure joy.

Everyone had a wonderful time. Even the Money-Pig made himself agreeable. He could still only eat soft food; it was whispered that he might have to live on cake for the rest of his days, and he certainly began now with such haste that Bulka had to drag him away, declaring that *some* must be left for the rest of the guests!

In a pause in the music Poor Cecco stood by Jensina, gazing on the happy throng.

'Isn't it nice?' he said. 'Oh, Jensina, how well everything has turned out! Look at Tubby! Look at Bulka, all over cake crumbs! Really, it almost makes one feel—'

'Yes?' murmured Jensina, gazing shyly up at him. She was thinking of what the policeman rat had said.

'– makes one feel like standing on one's head!' finished Poor Cecco somewhat hastily, for he had caught the look in Jensina's eye.

Jensina's natural common sense returned to her.

'You needn't think *I'm* in a hurry to get married, either,' she retorted instantly, 'because I'm not. I much prefer a life of adventure and combat!'

'And from what I know of you,' Poor Cecco gallantly returned, 'you're likely to get plenty of it! And now I must go and dance with Tubby!'

And with this he slipped away, just as the music struck up once more.

'Hey Presto!' said Harlequin.

THE END